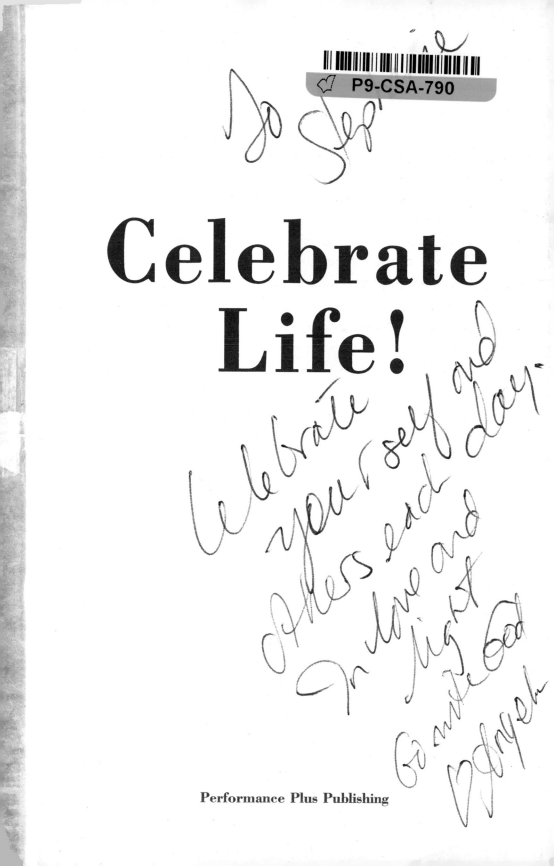

Celebrate Life!

Performance Plus Publishing

Celebrate Life!

Create the Life you Love to Live

ANGELA JACKSON

The author of this book does not dispense medical advice nor prescribe the use of any technique as a form of treatment for physical, emotional, or medical problems without the advice of a physician. The intent of the author is to offer general information that can help you help yourself. In the event that you use any information in this book for yourself, the author and publisher assume no responsibility for your actions.

Jackson, Angela Jude
    Celebrate life: create the life you love to live
ISBN 0-9696836-1-8
    1. Self-help techniques 2. Self-management (Psychology)
3. Spirituality I. Title

Inquiries should be addressed to:
Celebrate Life,
Performance Plus Publishing
2693 Lakeshore Boulevard West, Suite 11
Toronto, Ontario, Canada M8V 1G6

Editor: Katherine Coy
Cover design: Sarah Battersby
Author Photo: Andrew Clyde Little
Text design and page layout: Heidy Lawrance Associates

Printed in Canada by Webcom Ltd.

Visit Ms. Jackson's website: www.angelajackson.com

Table of Contents

Acknowledgements

I have deep gratitude for the following:

My Higher Power who guides me with a loving hand;

The 12-Step programs and the people who carry the message of these programs;

My partner Fraser, who accepts and loves me as I am;

My brother, my children and grandchildren, for being who they are;

My dear friend Dolce who tirelessly read the manuscript and offered valuable suggestions. Thanks also to Kay, Reva, Vivian and Lee for their time and their comments.

A special thank you to all the wonderful people who have attended my presentations and seminars, and to those who have written so many grateful letters about my first book *"Celebrating Anger."* Thank you for being so generous with your praise. Thank you for continuing to urge me to write this book. It took me a while, but here it is!

Finally, I want to acknowledge you, dear reader. Without you, there would be no reason to write.

Foreword

*That is what learning is. You suddenly
understand something you've
always understood all your life,
but in a new way.*
Doris Lessing

*Any love given freely, any work chosen with
passion, these are grand reasons
for celebration!*
Angela Jackson

Just like yours, my life has had its twists and turns, rather like
the child's game of snakes and ladders, up one moment, down
the next. I'm more than halfway through my life now, a good place
to pause and consider the view.

I've decided to regard my life as a work of art I'm in the process
of creating, which means I can stand apart from it and notice the
overall colours, the hues and textures. I can see the successes and
failures, revisit the longings and lessons, and observe a pattern and
direction. For the most part I like what I see, which doesn't mean
that I don't have regrets. Of course, there are black splotches on
my canvas; places I'd paint differently, patches I'd do over in hindsight. I suspect that most of us feel like this, even though we know

that if we could have done better, we would have. Overall, I see an interesting and creative life, fully lived. I can even trace a theme, weaving in and out, becoming stronger and more dominant as I step back and reflect.

> *Two roads diverged in a yellow wood,*
> *And sorry I could not travel both*
> *And be one traveler, long I stood*
> *And looked down one as far as I could*
> *To where it bent in the undergrowth;*
> *Then took the other, as just as fair,*
> *And having perhaps the better claim,*
> *Because it was grassy and wanted wear...*
> *Two roads diverged in a wood, and I—*
> *I took the one less traveled by.*
> Robert Frost

How I loved that poem. As a teen I read it over and over, committing it to memory, as if in so doing I would be able to follow the road and live happily ever after. It took me years to understand that no path is easy. Each of us has a road to walk and no one knows what the price and the payoffs will be.

I was also drawn to Edna St. Vincent Millay's words:

> *My candle burns at both its ends;*
> *It will not last the night;*
> *But ah, my foes and oh, my friends—*
> *It gives a lovely light.*

It seemed I was forever dancing, like moth to flame, towards the bright lights of material gratification—and destruction, through burning myself out—while at the same time yearning for spiritual contentment and inner peace. Like two lovers beckoning me, I couldn't choose one or the other, so I hovered around both.

This book is about celebrating the journey. The whole adventure of living.

I have written this book as a touchstone, to acknowledge what I've learned, and as a guideline, in the hope that it will ignite something in you. Perhaps it will throw off a spark to assist you in determining your life's theme; help you clarify your purpose, so that you can access your passion and let it burst within you, giving you the impetus to change direction, if that's necessary, or to fully embrace whatever it is you're chosen to make *your personal work of art.*

We get into trouble when we fail to recognize that we are in charge of our life experience. I think it's imperative that we stop living by rote and take time to survey what we're creating. The lessons of 9/11 reverberate: take time to decide what really matters—then prioritize sanely.

This book is intended to facilitate a reflective process. When we step back and look at our lives from a big-picture perspective, it seems easier to observe what's working and what isn't.

This book will assist you in accessing your inner landscape. It will also help you sort out your life purpose, and see where your growth areas lie. I have included personal stories, real-life examples and activities designed to help you self-explore. In the process, I hope you will discover that life is neither a confusing puzzle nor something to be managed. Life is simply a canvas, available to each of us, primed and ready for our creation. All we need to do is paint the magnificent and rich panorama of who and what we really are.

Metaphorically, I see each of us like a unique flower, here on earth for a brief speck of time, and our job is to bud and bloom for however long we have, and fulfill our individual destiny. To manage this, we need to have a firm stem connecting us to the earth. We need a good foundation, initially given or later developed, so that we can nurture our potential in deep rich soil. We need enough sun, water, air, food, laughter and love so we can grow upright, blossom vibrantly and fully occupy our space. When we have enough sustenance to grow ourselves, it's easy to sway toward the other flowers blooming around us, to merge without losing our essence. However, some flowers get nipped in the bud, or become withered and twisted, never emerging into their full radiance, while others extend their petals and sweet perfume for everyone to inhale. And so it is with us. Some of us curl up and hold onto self-limiting beliefs and destructive habits, which keep us stunted, while others burst forth vibrantly into full abundance.

Why is it that some people are able to bloom fully and others are not? How *can* we create the life we long to live? What do we need to do so we can live happy, joyous and free? These questions form the heart of this book, the trial-and-error version of a survivor; notes taken along the way.

I invite you to use whatever appeals to you as a palate for fashioning your own work of art. Try out the suggested Celebration Strategies found at the end of each chapter, use what feels right for you and leave the rest. Here's an overview of themes we will explore. A chapter is devoted to each theme.

1. Discover your path
2. Finish unfinished business
3. Release fear
4. Sweet surrender
5. Tame the inner tigers
6. Acceptance
7. Find forgiveness
8. Fulfill purpose
9. Love ourselves
10. Love others
11. Live healthy
12. Embrace death
13. Design your life
14. Celebrate!

On her 16th birthday, Jeanne Calmet told reporters the reason for her long and fulfilling life: "I never refused an opportunity to grow. No matter what was happening on life's highway, I figured if change was still requiring me to make adjustments, it meant God wasn't finished with me yet."

Since you and I are both still here, we know that change is forever tugging at us, enticing us to make those "adjustments." I still have a lot of learning to do, and each day opportunities whisper: come love, laugh, play, grow and learn.

I hope you will experiment with the ideas you encounter in these pages. I'm delighted that you're here and invite you to enjoy the journey.

One

Discover Your Path

**As long as you live,
keep learning how to live.**
Seneca

How do you like to celebrate? The last time you planned a celebration for someone or something, what did it involve? Most likely lots of choices: deciding on an event to celebrate, determining who to invite, making phone calls or sending out invitations, planning the menu, preparing food and drink and making sure you and your home were readied to put your best face on to receive guests. Now, of course the celebration probably threw some curves at you, maybe some guests were late or the food didn't turn out *quite* as you expected. Was it stressful? Maybe. Fun? Most definitely. Without your work, the celebration couldn't have taken place, and you wouldn't have been able to roll with the punches as easily as you did. Your life can be a grand celebration, if you choose to make it so. In this chapter, we are going to look at where to start when hosting the personal celebration that is our lives.

Why celebrate? Given the alternative, why not? Life is a feast, a banquet, resplendent with every imaginable colour, taste, scent and opportunity. Life, they say, is what we make of it. Which means we're the artists of our destiny, and we create the life we live. The question is: what do you think of your creation thus far? Is it all you want it to be? Is it a joyous creation? A life rich in imagination? Full of beauty? Are you living in abundance, experiencing vibrant health, doing work you are committed to and expressing your individuality? Do you have inner peace? A feeling of connection with all that's around you? Do you spend time with people who enrich your life? Are you in a relationship that helps you grow? Are you living on your own and liking it? Are you grateful for the myriad of gifts your life has brought you, especially the disappointments, struggles, mistakes and losses; the many times you've had to pick yourself up and lick your wounds? Those intense learning periods test our capacity to enjoy life, yet give us so much of what we need to learn.

Why is it that so many of us delay our living until we're faced with dying? "Live your life now!" my son-in-law's mother urged from her deathbed. "Don't wait! Take your trips now, do what's important. It's too late for me, but not for you!" She was only four years older than I am now. As I placed a red rose on her casket, her words echoed in my mind. "Live your life now!"

Why do so many of us get motivated only when we lose someone or are in a health crisis? Do we really think we have unlimited time, that our tomorrows stretch out ahead of us like a seemingly unending highway? Could that be the reason we hold back from living fully today?

Here's a tale about a young man named Jerry who died prematurely. He was an innocent fellow who had not been able to explore life as much as he wanted. He believed in heaven and hell, and knew he was on his way to heaven when his guide came to fetch him, but he was curious about hell, so he asked his guide if it were possible to get a glimpse of it on the way.

"No problem," answered his guide. "Let's get going."

Jerry was led through the doors of an old building, then down a long, dark, narrow hallway. Near the end of the hallway, the guide opened a heavy iron door. Peeking inside, Jerry saw a magnificent room, adorned with exquisite works of art and richly textured tapestries. Sunlight poured through large windows, and in the center of the room was a huge wooden table, overflowing with succulent, mouth-watering food. Hoards of people, dressed in beautiful clothes, were seated around the table. Looking closer, the young man noticed that inside their lovely clothes, the people were haggard and gaunt and had grim faces. In front of each person was a huge fork. Forks with handles so big they couldn't get the food from the table into their mouths and so, despite the bounty and beauty around them, they were starving.

"This is hell," the guide announced. "Take a good look."

Jerry was horrified by what he saw and was eager to move to heaven. Continuing their walk down the long hall, the guide opened another door.

"Welcome to heaven" he announced.

At first Jerry was perplexed. This room looked the same as the hellish one. Same magnificent paintings, same sun cascading through windows, same long banquet table piled high with succulent food, same big forks, but these people were laughing and robust. And then he noticed what they were doing. They were feeding one another. Jerry realized that the only difference between hell and heaven was that in heaven people helped one another.

I think it's the same on earth. When we give ourselves to others, we are in heaven. By sharing what we've got, be it pennies, pesos or pounds, we feel connected to our fellow beings. When we share our food, shelter, ideas and, most importantly, our time, we create a life that is heavenly.

Conversely, when we spend too much time in our own heads, in our own myopic world, our experience grows increasingly narrow and we create our hell.

St. Maria Ignatius had a near-death experience, and when she revived, she told this story to everyone who would listen: "I felt a beautiful warmth, saw a golden light, and heard a question. The question seemed to come at me from the inside and it was gentle but persistent. The question was: *how much love did you give?* I was at a loss. I realized I'd been stingy with my love. In that split second I resolved to love whomever crossed my path." You notice the question wasn't how much money did you make, or how much fame did you enjoy. It was how much love did you give.

Every day, millions of people routinely give their hope, their wisdom, their knowledge and their love to others. Usually this giving is not acknowledged publicly. It's not printed in the newspapers or noted in the Guinness Book of Records. The givers probably don't get much in the way of credit, but you know what? I think they're creating their own heaven on earth.

You and I have also given our love, our strength and our hope to others. That's when we feel good. And there are other times when we're stingy; when we isolate or cut ourselves off from one another. Times when we criticize each another; attack, blame and seek power over; dump on, hurt by thought or deed. Those are the times when we choose to live in hell. I know. I've been there.

The truth is that we create our own destiny. At any moment we can choose to live in heaven . . . or in hell.

We can do or be anything that we want to in life
William George Jackson

My father was my first profound teacher. I know he told the truth when he said the above words, because I've lived them. What he didn't tell me was that it takes effort to create the life you love to live. Effort and discipline. For a long time I thought I was "entitled;" that because I'd survived a traumatic childhood, the world owed me payback for the misery I'd endured. I didn't think this on a conscious level, but it was manifested in my attitude. Have you ever thought that because you had paid dearly at some time in your life, you were owed?

In my life fantasy, I thought I was supposed to be compensated, and eventually restored to my throne. Me—the exiled princess. It didn't happen. I waited for the prince to arrive and when he did, I noticed his warts. Traded him in for another. More warts. Each of my relationships and all of my jobs had glitches. Nothing was as I thought it should be. Even my kids didn't do what I wanted.

I seemed to go from hope to expectancy to disappointment without ever understanding why.

Through making the same mistakes over and over again until I was sick and tired of being sick and tired, I was finally able to stop doing what wasn't working and do something different. Today I know life isn't fair, it is simply life. Like those people feeding one another, I have learned to find contentment by taking care of myself with one hand and giving to others with the other. To count my blessings and stay grateful for what I have.

Life is like a hand of cards. We get what we're dealt and we have to play with what we've got. We don't receive a blueprint, a guideline for living when we're born. We have to make one up or whistle in the dark as we go along. Well I suspect I've finally got the blueprint and I'm eager to share what I've learned with you.

When you hosted or attended your last celebration, once the guests arrived at the door, did the hosts turn off all the lights and leave? Did the hosts serve food that they hated? Of course not, it would have been at cross-purposes with the goal of the party! If we wouldn't do this for a party, then why would we do it for our life's celebration? We need to take a clear look at how we undermine and sabotage ourselves, and resolve to do what is necessary to make adjustments and create the life we love to live. I have discovered that, like planning a celebration, in order to fully participate in the adventure of living, we need to determine what is working in our lives and then release what is not. Below are some statements that can serve as reference points as you travel on your journey of celebration. If you are ready to begin this process, grab a pen and respond to the following statements as truthfully as possible.

Celebration Strategies
Your Personal Assessment

Please circle the word that best represents your experience with each of the following sentences

1. **I make time to let go, play and be silly with my partner or friends.**
   high   medium   low
2. **I frequently laugh with my friends and colleagues.**
   high   medium   low
3. **I communicate effectively in highly charged emotional situations.**
   high   medium   low
4. **I have an abundance of love in my life.**
   high   medium   low
5. **I listen to others without wanting to finish their sentences, change the subject or tune out.**
   high   medium   low
6. **I take time for physical/mental/spiritual/emotional nurturing.**
   high   medium   low

7. I use positive affirmations or visualizations to maintain my self-confidence.

high   medium   low

8. My moments of frustration are short-lived.

high   medium   low

9. I am able to handle stressful situations without becoming stressed.

high   medium   low

10. I feel content and peaceful most of the time.

high   medium   low

11. I am presently living the life I love to live.

high   medium   low

12. In my twilight years I can imagine looking back over my life and being grateful for the choices I have made.

high   medium   low

13. If this was my last day on earth, I would consider my life a success.

high   medium   low

14. I believe it is possible to have it all.

high   medium   low

15. I am ready to have it all.

high   medium   low

Your answers have earned the following points for each response. High = 3, Medium = 2, Low = 1.

A. Statements 1 to 5 are about the quality of relationships and interpersonal communication skills.

B. Statements 6 to 10 refer to how well you take care of your mental, emotional and physical health needs.

C. Statements 11 to15 are quality of life indicators.

There is a total of 15 points available in each of the categories A through C.

Did any of your answers surprise you? If you have been truth-ful with your answers, and scored between 11 and 15 in a category, you are doing very well, so congratulate yourself! If you scored between 7 and 10, you are making progress, so give yourself a pat on the back and keep on going. If you scored below 7, know that you are not alone and that you've made a step in the right direc-tion. Continue on and try out the recommended activities in each chapter and you just might find some reasons to begin celebrating.

The way I see it, each one of us is a blessed event just because we're here. No matter what else happens, we're alive breathing beings, living on planet earth, fully equipped for life. And each one of us is a miracle, a cause for celebration. If you haven't yet cele-brated your arrival on earth, why not do so now, this very minute. Give yourself a big cheer, and say "hooray for me, I'm here." You can herald your emergence anytime because it's better to do it later than never to welcome yourself at all. Hooray for you, you're here! When we are able to honour our existence, it's easier to walk our truest path.

In the next few chapters we'll be looking at what we need to do to make sure that we stay on track with knowing who we really are and honouring our existence. To do this we may need to pull up a few weeds and create more space, that is, examine how we sabo-tage our best intentions and resolve to change our patterns; see where our beliefs keep us stunted and get rid of them. Then we need to roll up our sleeves and get to work—use the tools that enable us to live consciously. That way we can blossom fully and totally occupy the space and time we have on earth. One of the first tools we'll be using is affirmations. Affirmations are truth builders—seeds sown inside that need to be watered repeatedly for healthy growing. An affirmation is a simple statement that affirms our basic worth. It needs to be short and to the point, written in the present tense with positive language. It helps to include your name. For example:

Affirmation: I _____ *(your name)*
am grateful that I was born. Hoorah for me, I am here.

Two

Finish Unfinished Business

*Before sunlight can shine through a
window, the blinds must be raised.*
American Proverb

The past is never dead; it isn't even past.
William Faulkner

Today I give keynote presentations in which I talk, share
stories, sing and enjoy my audience. One of my biggest life
lessons has been that in order to be all I can be, I needed to free
myself from my own traps. In order to give and receive all I can in
life, I have to acknowledge what is holding me back and let it go.
In my case it was resentment and fear. I needed to journey back-
wards to clear my pathway. I had to finish my unfinished business.

Once upon a time, a little girl was born to a couple that had
waited many years to have her. For her first six years she had a cozy
home, two loving parents, and a sense of belonging. Bright-eyed and
curious, this little girl loved the sunshine and was forever running
outside, twirling in her back yard, dancing in the summer light,
squishing the brown mud through her toes, and throwing herself

into the green grass to smell the earth. Life was her playground. Her closest friend was Scotty Gormley[1] who lived one block away. Inseparable, they would talk and play and dream together.

In the girl's home there was warmth and the sound of piano music wafting through the air like colourful ribbons. She could tell what was going on by the sound of this music. Sometimes it was thunderous and fierce, other times it was tinkling and merry, happy trills gaily played by her beautiful mother who smelled like flowers. Then there was the sad music, which penetrated the little girl's heart and she felt sad without knowing why.

The girl admired her mother and adored her father. Her magnificent tall red-headed father who smiled at her from his light green eyes and told her he loved her. Although he travelled a lot, when he came home it was magic. Up in the air he would swing her, higher than all the furniture, then he would plunk her on top of his broad shoulders. And there she would sit, surveying the world. Sometimes she would reach up her hand and touch the ceiling. The miracle of being able to touch the ceiling!

"Sweetheart, you can be or do anything you want to in this life," her father would tell her, as they travelled from room to room. "You're my princess and the sky's the limit!"

I was that little girl. In those days I believed I really was a princess and thought my father was the king. Although I loved my mother, sometimes she seemed more like a wicked witch, particularly when she'd wash out my mouth with soap and make me stand in the corner and think about how bad I'd been.

My brother Nick was born when I was five, and after a few months of fierce jealousy I began to love him too. You may well think that this is another boring story of a person who had it all, but hang in. First impressions may not always be the long lasting truth, for while I started life in a cozy setting; I had to go through many thorny experiences before I found my path.

---

1 Not his real name

When I was six, my golden ladder became a treacherous slide and down, down, down I fell, like Alice, only there was no wonderland below. My father disappeared. Pouf! Just like that. One day he was there and the next day he was gone. Later, I heard he'd run off to California with a young movie starlet. My mother was left to take care of me and my little brother Nick, a task she could not handle, and so the house was let go and the toys were given up. Friends, school and all things familiar disappeared, including my brother and me.

After finding a job and a one-bedroom apartment, my mother placed Nick and me in separate foster homes. Foster homes in Montreal during the 1940s were largely unsupervised and designed to bring additional income to the foster parents, who could use children as unpaid workers. If you've seen the movie *Oliver*, you'll have a picture of what it was like.

After school l spent hours scrubbing floors, polishing windows, cleaning counters and trying to avoid those daily beatings. Surviving abuse during the next seven years became my mission. Some of the lessons I learned then have taken me a long way. Lessons like:

- Rely on yourself. If you want to make something happen, then do it.
- There is nothing that won't pass. No matter how bad or how good it is, nothing lasts forever.
- Dream dreams, and make them big ones! Dreams carry you through those awful snake pit times.
- If at first you don't succeed, try, try again. Persevere!

I also learned some other lessons that weren't so good, lessons I've had to unlearn and replace with new ones:

- Don't trust anyone.
- Don't ask for anything. Take it instead.
- When you're scared, hold your breath and pretend you're invisible.

Back then I dreamed about being a singer, an actress. As a teenager I added being a teacher and a writer. I wanted all of these things, and I couldn't imagine achieving any one of them. Yet my early lessons of self-reliance, dreaming big and persevering have paid off, for in my life I've been a teacher, a writer and today I make my living talking—quite an irony when you consider how my mother used to tell me to be seen but not heard.

My Journey of Liberation

When I was six years old and dumped at that first bleak foster home, I was in shock and terrified. Later came the agony of loss. I couldn't understand what had happened. Maybe my mother had told me something, had hinted at a reason for the sudden move, but I had no recollection of it. One moment I'd had a home, a mommy, a daddy, and a baby brother and the next moment I didn't. One morning I was safe and protected because I was part of a family, and by evening I was alone and exposed and part of nothing. In the blink of an eye, the flick of a wrist, my world changed.

I didn't understand any of it. All I could surmise was that somehow I had done something terribly, unforgivably wrong, something so dreadful that this was my punishment. I thought it would end. I was sure my mother would come and take me away from the dark, loveless, dingy place with the mean old ladies. I was sure she'd return and tell me it was all a big mistake and the sentence was over. Every day I waited for her, watching from my little window, believing she would come.

At the end of two weeks I saw her from my watching post, saw her pretty blue and white polka dot dress billowing around her legs and her chestnut curls bouncing in the breeze. At last, my beautiful mother had come for me. Eagerly I bolted down the stairs and flew out the door, running to greet her, to smell her and feel her close to me.

"I have only two hours to visit with you and Nick," my mother said, "so we have to move quickly and go pick him up."

What does that mean, two hours to visit? How do you visit with your mother and brother for two hours? What do you say? How can relationships survive on two hours a week?

I don't know what these visits were like for her. For me they were water in the desert. I spent every day of each lonely week longing for her and waiting for the punishment to end. Those visits, the tiny bits of contact, became nirvana. And a ritual. Sunday afternoons my mother would pick me up, we'd get on a bus and go to the foster home where Nick was living, and then we'd go to the park, or sit in a restaurant. I don't remember our conversations. I do remember watching my mother push my brother in the swing, watching from the sidelines, hearing him laugh as he went up and down, feeling an immense sadness well up in me, then pushing it back down again.

Big Girls Don't Cry

Gradually it dawned on me that this was now my life. I lived in a dark and lonely place with people who didn't speak to me, who didn't love me. I believed it was because I'd been bad. Bad, bad, bad. So I scrubbed floors and washed dishes. I was seen and not heard. An observer instead of a participant. Obedient to others, at least on the outside. Desperate on the inside.

Gradually I became a bigger girl wearing a false face—an "I'm fine" mask. I disassociated from my despair and developed bravado instead of confidence. Convinced I was unlovable, I pretended I was a princess in disguise, waiting. Someday he would rescue me, my father, the handsome king. By now I knew my mother was not going to, so I transferred my hopes onto my father, waiting for him to arrive.

By age 10 I was living in my fourth foster home. While this home was generally better than the others, there was one big problem. Archie, my foster father, began to make a habit of coming for me on "our Wednesdays" as he called them. After Muriel, his wife, went bowling, he'd take me by the hand and lead me to his bedroom. After what seemed like a long time, Archie would tell me I could go, but first he make me promise not to tell anyone or else . . . *his finger ran across my throat* . . . and I knew what that meant . . . he'd kill me.

I kept the promise for about a year. One day I told a classmate, who told her mother, who called Archie's wife, who called in the social worker. She came to the house with my mother. They took me to the upstairs bathroom where they both told me I'd have to apologize for the terrible lies I'd been telling. When I tried to explain, the social worker told me to be quiet, to go downstairs and apologize.

When a child learns that the truth is not valued, she starts to deny her own experience. When a child is invalidated, she begins to invalidate herself.

I did not understand that the grown-ups were fearful. I thought I was bad and deserved my punishment. I slunk around in shame, wanting to hide, to cut off my head.

And then, miraculously, my father appeared. He drove up in small white convertible, with a pretty dark haired lady sitting beside him. "I've come to take you with me" he said. What sweet words! I ran inside and threw my belongings into my battered brown suitcase.

Off we drove, gaily singing songs and playing "I spy with my little eye" and "20 Questions." Finally we parked at the end of a long driveway in a town called Peterborough, in the province of Ontario. I'd never been to Ontario before, never been outside of Montreal. My dad and Margie, his new wife, led me into a brightly lit small bungalow. Pretty yellow curtains framed the windows. The furniture was all white with flowered cushions on the couch and chairs. I had my very own bedroom for the first time in years, and on the bed sat a smiling teddy bear.

My dad bought a blond cocker spaniel puppy. We named the pup Nipper, because he nipped at our ankles. My mom sent me a bike and I rode that bike as if it were my horse, a wild steed. I felt as free as the wind, riding my bike after school. Saturdays were special because I'd go to movie matinees with my dad and Margie. Life was beautiful!

Deep woods surrounded our little house and I was eager to explore them. Often I'd take Nipper and go to the woodland fort I'd made out of broken logs and stones. There I would read and daydream and tell Nipper my secrets.

At night I'd do my homework by the fireplace. Then I'd take a bath and when I finished, I'd push back the empty brown bottles that had rolled out from underneath the tub. In bed I'd cuddle with Nipper and fall into a sound sleep, knowing I was safe and loved at last.

One day I met two boys, classmates of mine, on the way home. They said they wanted to be friends and asked if they could come to my house and play a game. I was excited. No one had wanted to play games or be my friend. Proudly I showed them the fort I'd built. I was 10 and they were probably 11 years old. "Okay, you lie down, and Tim will lie on you and I'll count how many times he fucks you," said Joel, the older boy. I don't think any of us knew what the word meant. Wanting to be friends, I lay down with all my clothes on and Tim lay on top of me and Joel counted: "I fuck you once, I fuck you twice" as Tim pushed his hips up then down on mine. When he got to 50 they changed positions. At the end of this ritual we still had all of our clothes on, yet I felt dirty.

That night I told my dad and Margie about the game. They looked at one another and were silent. Later my dad took me by the hand to Joel's home, and told me to wait on the sidewalk while he knocked on Joel's door. I was frightened; I didn't know what would happen. Fearing I'd be punished because I had told, I waited anxiously.

Joel's dad came to the door, I heard the murmur of conversation, then my dad came back to the sidewalk and took my hand and we walked home in silence. We never spoke about that incident but I felt lighter, as if some piece of a puzzle I didn't understand had been put into place. I didn't feel as ugly. A bit of shame had been lifted through my dad's actions.

We'd been living in Peterborough for about a year when my dad disappeared. There was no warning, no goodbye. Two blue pawn tickets lay on top of his bureau. One was for the antique doll my mother had given me, and the other was for my bike.

Margie put me on a train bound for Montreal. My mother put me in another foster home, and life went on.

When a child is moved from home to home, from person to person, she loses a little more of herself with each move.

She doesn't know where she belongs, or with whom. I waited for my dad to come back, but he never did. I moved into three more foster homes between the ages of 11 and 13.

The Past is Always Present

The past is but the beginning of a beginning.
H.G. Wells

Wherever we go, we take ourselves with us. I will never be able to go back and create a different past for myself, or regain those lost years. And yet, I have learned to use the past to understand myself better. I have also used the past to understand others. When we use our past experience creatively, instead of using it to justify our behaviour or to blame others, we really can create a new future. When we finish our unfinished business, we can create a wonderful now. A Wow Now! A heaven on earth.

Near our summer cottage in northern Ontario there's a big tree overhanging the Muskoka River. One branch of the tree has a rope dangling from it, from which kids swing out and jump into the dark river below. Many times I hear their young voices shrieking, "I can't!" before they let go of the rope, then the laughter comes, when they bob up from the water, proudly realizing they've done it. What courage it takes to let go and travel where we haven't gone before!

Finishing unfinished business is like that rope swing. First we need to stand our ground and survey what we've got to work with. Like those kids, we need to look down at the water below. Then we need to take a chance, grab onto the rope, swing out and trust that it will hold us. Believe that the rope is strong; have faith that the water won't disappear. We need to know that we're not going to perish when we let go of the rope. Which means having courage, trusting the process, then doing it. Actually letting go.

One could do worse than be
a swinger of birches
Robert Frost

What an exhilarating experience. And it doesn't matter what our issues are, the process is the same. In dealing with our challenges we might find ourselves in "murky waters." So it's important to do the research first. To search out the right person(s) to share with: a therapist, friend or self-help group. Then we need to . . . just do it. Claim our past, feel our anguish and pain, share our sad secrets, empty our bucket of self-pity. Revisit all of it . . . then . . . let it go.

For some, this process might mean sitting quietly, taking a trip down memory lane and allowing feelings to surface. Others might want to write out recollections in a journal. If you haven't done this before, you can start by writing for a minimum of 10 minutes each day, ignoring the temptation to chronicle your doings. Just write whatever comes up for you, concentrating on your feelings. Once you've developed the habit of journaling you might want to write about your history. You could research your family tree, looking for patterns and clues. Then you could write your own story, focusing on what you would prefer to avoid. That's where the gold is.

Examine Your History

Begin by asking yourself what you've been avoiding. What have you put "on hold" in your life? What have you not looked at? Write your story, and then read it aloud. By seeing it on paper and hearing yourself say the words, you'll start to reclaim the part of yourself and your history that you've abandoned. Whatever your inner journey is, I urge you to begin taking it, believing that all will be well. And it will be, eventually.

We can choose to put closure on our past, to finish our unfinished business, then use it as rich compost for our own fertile fields. That way it becomes foundation soil from which to create new beginnings. Everything that happened to us gets viewed as a necessary ingredient, which, when used appropriately, can bring forth a bountiful harvest.

I have been able to take events that once caused me anguish and extract profound learning from them. I use this knowledge when I'm giving workshops or counselling others. Every loss I've had has become a gain in compassion and understanding. Today I am grateful for each painful experience I have survived. They are gems I adorn myself with, jewels that have strengthened me and enabled me to be the person I now am. I've learned that blessings and tragedies visit us all and because of my early losses I can help others deal with theirs.

I'm not saying the past evaporates. It never does. What happens is that it loosens its hold on us, and we can step out of bondage. A wise therapist once told me, "there is no end to the primal scream, we all want to be perfectly loved. It isn't possible, but there is an end to the crying out for it."

Finishing unfinished business is a great adventure! I've travelled in many countries, but none so rewarding as my internal trip. How do we get going? By becoming willing to begin. Take the first step. Unpack the suitcase. The perfect time to start is now; there will never be a better moment. Remember, the past does not equal the future.

We *can* break patterns and change the course of our lives. You too can put your past to rest.

Now is the time to begin the activity section of this chapter. You might want to use a special notebook and pen to do your activities. Find a place to work where you won't be interrupted. If you want to create a ritual, try lighting a candle and playing soft music. Or just relax into a comfortable chair. Here are some strategies to help you begin.

Celebration Strategies

Unpack Your Suitcase

1. **Take out a fresh notebook. Write on the top**
   Finishing my unfinished business.
   Breathe deeply. Exhale.
2. **Start by writing out the following question on the left side of your page.**
   Who am I?

Draw one line down the middle of your paper; write out this question on the left side and write in answers on the right. Write the question over and over again and respond with whatever answer comes up. Remember, there is no wrong answer!

Do this 20, 50, 100 times, until you feel complete.

For example:

Who am I?	*I'm me*
Who am I?	*I'm a person*
Who am I?	*I'm a parent*
Who am I?	*I'm angry*
Who am I?	*I'm a writer*
Who am I?	*I'm scared*
Who am I?	*I'm a woman/man*

Don't worry about repetition. If you get stuck just repeat what you last said until you get to a new place. Let whatever comes come. Just keep asking the question and recording the answer. You can use a computer if you want to, although you'll get more out of this activity by writing. Just do it over and over until you feel empty, until you feel you have nothing left to say.

Then take a stretch break before you move on to the next question. Or set up another appointment with yourself.

3. What part of me have I left behind? What part of me have I "disowned?"

For example, I disowned the abandoned child. I disowned the defenseless, sad little girl I once was. I disowned the child I thought was bad. Turned my back on my dependent self, on my vulnerability. I created a strong facade, an "I'm in charge" persona. I even shed my name, which used to be Jude. I called myself Angela. I did not want to have any part of that pathetic, loveless child. So I buried her. And along with that burial I killed my inventive, spontaneous self too. Funny how that works. You can't just get rid of the unwelcome parts; it's a package deal. And although I had a good "cover," I was not authentically me.

How about you? What have you pushed aside? Here is your opportunity to find out!

4. What is your "unfinished business?"

Allow yourself to sit with this question. Give yourself time to mull it over. Then start writing or doodling, drawing, or talking into a tape recorder. Let whatever comes, come. Accept what there is. If you get stuck, then write or draw with your non-dominant hand because that hand reflects your intuitive side. We each know what we need to work on; all we have to do is give it time and permission to surface.

Put the telephone on hold. Shut down the computer. Minimize distractions and stay present with yourself.

You may experience some sadness or anger, but remember, "no pain = no gain." You will survive this, and you will be amazed at the freedom you experience once you are through. Because *the only way out is through!*

5. How can I finish?

What do you need to do about what you have uncovered? Could you write a letter? You don't have to send it, just write one to whomever you have unfinished business with. That's a good start. Ask yourself "How can I put closure on this?" Repeat the question to yourself, stay with it, and live in the question for as long as you need. Let yourself walk around with it, write it out, put it under your pillow, and sleep on it. Remember you have allies, people who can help you with this part. Grab onto the rope!

For example, I needed to let go of my dream that my family would come together again. My dad would not reappear, my brother would not move in, and no one was going to come and rescue me. I needed to accept that my mom couldn't express her love any better than she did. I needed to understand that my parents weren't able to give me a foundation of security on which I could later stand. This was a painful realization, one I had to sit with for a while and truly experience, before the healing tears could begin.

Once I was able to give up the dream, I could accept what I had in front of me, which meant that I could let go of my fantasy of the perfect family and enjoy what I had. I know my parents did the best they could. But facts are facts. Facing the truth gave me freedom and helped me to bury the dream that I had projected onto every relationship I'd had. Does our unfinished business ever end? Perhaps not, but as the load gets lighter, the unmanageable becomes manageable. When you are able to accept that the past does not equal the future, you will experience an openness within you, a space that hasn't been available for a while. Nurture this space, let it grow.

6. Use an affirmation.
For example,

I, Angela Jude, am a much loved child of God.

I used this affirmation to help me understand that I had divine parenting, and was worth loving. To affirm that God, which I see as loving energy and the spirit of the universe, made me, and I am not junk. If you don't like the word God, then substitute another, it's only a word after all.

It strengthens the affirmation when you put your name after the "I." Then you can speak your affirmation, sing it, dance it, or write it out over and over again in your very best handwriting. You could record it and listen to your own voice affirming you. Say it first thing in the morning and last thing at night. There are endless possibilities of words you could choose to use. For example,

I _____ am willing to complete my unfinished business.

or

I _____ am willing to believe I am loveable.

If these are not the right affirmations for you, then create ones that are. You'll see big pay-offs when you repeat your affirmation on a regular basis. Guaranteed.

You have done a lot of deep work in these activities, so remember to give yourself a hug or a pat on the back, and tell yourself how proud you are of you. By looking at the past you've taken a giant step forward in your journey. You are no longer lost in the woods alone, for you've begun to clear a pathway that will lead you to freedom. Keep your eye on the clearing ahead!

Affirmation: I am willing to be free. I am willing to complete my unfinished business.

Three

Release Fear

Beyond this place of wrath and fear,
looms but the horror of the shade,
and yet the menace of the years,
finds, and shall find me, unafraid.
Invictus

I have invented the world I see.
A Course in Miracles

Most of my life I've been afraid and didn't even know it. I covered up my fear with bravado, and thought I was courageous! Fear is what drove a lot of my decision-making and behaviours, although I never realized it. Only after identifying, naming and facing my fears was I able to overcome them and start living my life as a celebration instead of something to simply survive or get through.

By the time I was nine, I had been living in foster homes for two years. My mother got a job cooking on a small ranch for the summer, and she found a nearby home where my brother and I could stay. It was a paradise summer, because Nick and I were together again and free to act like the children we were.

We stayed with the Fourniers, an old French Canadian couple who had a few acres of farmland and a deserted barn for us to play in. How we loved pretending there were cows in the barn, and that we were the farmers! We swam in the nearby river and made friends with the local kids. They didn't speak English, and we couldn't speak much French, but we managed to communicate nonetheless.

Saturday nights were musical events. Friends and relatives would pile into the Fourniers' home. Soon the fiddle, harmonica, pots and spoons would come out, a toe-tapping rhythm would begin and before long, everyone was singing and making music, including us! I had many happy memories of our stay with this foster family.

One day, I got a bright idea. I decided that we kids would fly from the top beam of the old barn; if Peter Pan and Wendy could do it, why not us? It was to be a heroic feat; we would just spread our arms and fly. I don't know why flying appealed so much to me, but I really believed we could do it if we just got up high enough. Somehow, I convinced the other kids to climb up the rickety ladder and line up on the top beam of the big old barn. There we were, six little kids standing in a row on the highest wooden beam, too scared to look down at the hay way below.

I couldn't lose face!

It was my job to call out the signal: *"Un, deux, trois."* Nobody moved. They all stood there, looking at me. Then, I understood: it was my idea, so I was supposed to go first! Yikes! That was not what I had in mind. I thought we'd go together. Maybe this was not such a good idea after all, but what was I to do? I couldn't lose face, couldn't show my fear. So, with pounding heart, I raised my arms, perched on my tippy toes, took a step off the beam and flew in the air . . . for at least three seconds before making a painful crash landing in the hay.

My left arm was twisted beneath my back, broken in two places. The doctor said I was lucky I hadn't broken my neck. The Fourniers didn't want to be responsible for me anymore, and I was sent back to the city, to another dismal foster home—all because I was afraid to show fear.

Years later, I'm up on another high beam, only this time it's the beam of public speaking. My first attempt was terrifying as I wondered what had prompted me to think I could do it, convinced that people didn't want to hear anything I would say. I stood there, mute, certain I was about to make the biggest mistake of my life, wanting to run. Instead, I opened my mouth, and out came, *"I'm so nervous, it's a miracle that I'm actually standing because my knees are knocking together and my heart is pounding, and I wonder if any of you have ever felt like this?"* Nods of agreement, smiles, even chuckles came forth, and I began to relax. Because I was able to admit my fear and share it, I was able to move on from it.

Have you ever felt the kind of nervousness that makes your hands shake and your heart beat so fast you think it might fly right out of your chest? It has been years since I gave my first presentation, but I want you to know that each time I get up on a stage, I'm nervous. The difference is that now I turn this fear into exhilaration. I shake out my body and say a little prayer before I start, asking for guidance. Then I take in a deep breath, look into peoples' eyes, and begin. *I still feel fear* but there is a difference in how I handle it. Instead of being victimized by it, I notice the feeling, take a deep breath, exhale slowly, and do what's in front of me to do. In other words I manage fear rather than allow it to manage me.

Fear is a Four-letter Word

Fear has been around for a long time; we all experience it. Fear can serve us, if we let it. Fear can show us where we need to grow, or what we need to tackle. On a rudimentary level, fear lets us know when we're in danger. Our ancestors lived with fear every day as they went out to search for food. I wonder if they prayed first?

We experience fear as our jobs diminish and inflation increases; as the stock market dips and our savings dwindle. As terrorists and suicide bombers make headlines and war becomes routine. We may not fear wild animals today, but we live with untreatable diseases and skyrocketing costs of health care. We have longer life spans and less time. We know we need to protect our health, look after our investments, and put worry on the back burner, but do we? Aren't we plagued by imaginary fears such as: *"Will I be able to keep my job? Can I pay all these bills? Does my partner still love me? Will my kids be able to resist drugs?"* These fears sap our energy and take up precious headspace.

Managing Fear

The autumn I turned 17, I learned a valuable technique to deal with fear. My brother, Nick, was the catalyst. He was 12 at the time. Nick was on the roof of our apartment building playing catch with a boy on the roof of an adjacent apartment building. Nick missed the ball and caught the high-tension wire instead. Electricity surged through his right arm and came out through his knees, which were grounded against the ledge of the roof. The force of it hurled him off the building, sending him down four stories where his fall was softened by the bushes before he hit the concrete. For months he was in a coma, using an iron lung to breathe. No one knew if he would live or die.

During that time I experienced acute anxiety. I was terrified that my brother, whom I loved deeply—a love made more poignant by the fact that we had only lived together for the briefest time—would die. I was afraid that I would lose him and the only way I could deal with this anxiety was to walk and breathe, walk and breathe.

Eva, my best friend, would often accompany me on these walks, especially during those first hard nights. She kept on talking, telling me it was going to be all right, and we'd walk and breathe and talk and walk. I still use this technique today. When frightened, I breathe deeply, talk myself down and, as quickly as possible, share my fears with a trusted friend. It works. If I can go for a walk it's even better.

My brother did live and eventually recovered. His right arm was amputated at the forearm and he was told he'd never walk again. Today he is a marathon runner and makes his living programming computers. He's also a good carpenter. We have a close relationship, even though we live on separate continents. Although his accident had serious consequences, he has not let it stop him from experiencing a full life. And it gave me a good lesson in managing fear. I learned that none of us has to whistle alone in the dark.

Fears are Meant to be Spoken out Loud

Why is it so hard to admit fear? Why do we hold on to our "I'm fine" bluster with determination and clenched jaw? How come we have such a hard time admitting we don't know what we're doing half the time and that we're not really not the experts we pretend to be? I think it's because we're afraid we'll be judged and found wanting. We keep wearing the "I'm fine" mask even when it gets too tight for our faces. Then our chests get constricted and it becomes harder to breathe. Many of us end up having high blood pressure and heart attacks, which probably come from fear in the first place. What we need to realize is that experiencing fear is a natural part of living, and when we share our fearful feelings with others, the fear evaporates.

In a newspaper interview Stuart McLean, author of *Stories from the Vinyl Café* discussed how he learned to handle fear. At the time he was taking an applied social science course at Montreal's Concordia University (in those days it was called Sir George

Williams). "We studied group behaviour by studying our own group, so it was therapeutic, and I had a moment in one of those sessions where I expressed my fear about something and the leader said: 'Yeah, that must have been scary for you'. And in that moment, I felt I had finally been heard. And it was like the sky had cleared."

When our fears are heard and our feelings validated, we can let them go.

Doug, a counsellor I know, has a business card that reads: "Reasonably accurate advice." I like that phrase. It takes smugness out of the expert role and it gives him breathing room. Perhaps we can follow Doug's example and start realizing that no one has all the answers, yet together we have it all.

Earlier this summer I signed up for a two-day painting course in fluid acrylics—my virgin attempt at painting. The scariest moment was looking at that big white piece of paper and thinking *"What on earth am I going to put on it?"*—that initial moment where there is space and the unknown. Boldly, I splashed bright red on the paper. Naturally, there were moments of fear after I put that first stroke of daring colour down, moments where I thought, *"What if this is a big mistake, and I ruin the whole thing? I don't really know what I'm doing."* Yet, as long as I kept breathing and trusting the process, the painting seemed to work.

My Fear List

Sometimes I handle fear by writing out a fear list. This gets those niggly, nagging fears out of me and onto paper where I can see them. Perhaps you'd like to compare notes with me and see if your fears are similar.

- I'm afraid of getting old and disabled, old and sick, and in constant pain.
- I fear losing my loved ones, my friends and my pets.

- When I'm driving on the highway and there are a lot of big trucks to pass, I scare myself by thinking the trucks will overpower me.
- When my cat comes prancing towards me with a chipmunk in his mouth, I scream and run away.
- I'm afraid I won't have enough money to live on when I am old.

Most of my fears are centered on loss. After I make my fear list, I put it in my Fear Box—an old candy box I have reserved for this purpose. I say a prayer, then imagine all my fears rocketing up to a loving God who will handle them for me. Then I get busy. I pick up the spade and bury the dead animal. I drive defensively, leaving plenty of room for the trucks to pass. I call a financial advisor. In other words, I take care of what I can and leave the rest alone.

As for the fear of dying, although I haven't had much practice dealing with death, I know there's support available, a hand to hold, and people to learn from. I watch how others handle the loss of loved ones. I try to be there for them. It's all part of living this great adventure, isn't it?

Worry

I've taken to saying that worry comes from from **F**alse **E**xpectations **A**ppearing **R**eal or **F.E.A.R.** What I've learned about fear is that the imaginings are worse than the realities. It's **F.E.A.R** of fear that gets me scared and keeps me that way. All those "what if's" or "should have's" we think before or after the fact. Those negative ruminations that cause us worry and loss of sleep. The thing about worry is that it's useless; a complete waste of energy. It never solves a thing, and it keeps us stuck in a state of anxiety. The opposite of fear is faith and faith implies trusting. We can't have faith unless we trust.

When I get in worry mode, I practise letting go by exhaling deeply. Then I send my worries to my Higher Power. I put them in an imaginary red balloon and send them up beyond the clouds. When they're gone I try not to grab them back again! Here's some Irish wisdom.

There are two things to worry about.
Either you're well or you're sick.
If you're well, then there's nothing to worry about.
But, if you're sick, there are two things to worry about.
Either you will get well or you will die
If you get well, there's nothing to worry about.
If you die, there are only two things to worry about.
Either you will go to Heaven or Hell.
If you go to Heaven, there's nothing to worry about.
But, if you go to Hell, you'll be so damn busy shaking hands
with friends, you won't have time to worry!"
                    Cuala Press, County Clare, Ireland

When I feel scared and alone in the dark, I tell myself it's okay, I really am safe. I no longer live in foster homes, and nothing bad is going to happen. I cuddle with my cat or my teddy when my partner is away. I listen to a meditation tape to help relax.

Using deep breathing has been immensely beneficial for me. I used to have a brittle body. My shoulders were tight and poised. I was a good little soldier, marching with head erect, rigid, ready for battle. Now I let my shoulders soften and remind myself to breathe from my belly. When I concentrate on breathing, I'm able to let go of protective armor, and assess the situation calmly. It gives me time to pause. Then I can use my fear-releasing techniques. They work for me, and they can help you.

Celebration Strategies

Techniques for Releasing Fear

1. Allow fear to surface

The next time you're afraid, *feel it*. Locate the fear spot. Is it in your jaw, your neck, your belly? Is your heart pounding? Experience the sensation, savour it, acknowledge it. Then ask yourself, *"Is this fear about the present or the past?"* Often, our fears have nothing to do with today; when we recognize this, we can let them go.

2. Use your breath

Let your breathing calm your mind. Take several deep breaths, making sure each breath comes from your belly and not your chest. Concentrate on expanding your belly, then contracting it as you exhale. Deep breathing soothes both mind and body.

3. Release tension

Release tension in your shoulders by rolling them forward and back. Bring your right ear towards your right shoulder. Now, do the same with your left ear. Alternate ear-to-shoulder stretches. Breathe.

4. Get a worry basket

Find a basket or a box with a lid. Write each of your worries on a separate piece of paper, put them in the basket and attach the lid. Leave them there. In a few weeks or months you can open up the lid, survey the contents, and enjoy a good laugh.

The good part of fear is that it can be a warning signal, like seeing a driver coming out of an unexpected lane, or getting a notice that your electricity is going to be cut off. You can immediately do something about it. If there is real danger, look after yourself. Do what you need to do. Make the call, get out of the way, and change your situation. The vast majority of fears, however, are about petty concerns like, "Will I make it to _____ on time?" Or, they are about future worries, like, "What will happen if I lose my job or if this relationship ends?" It's fear of loss, plain and simple.

What I have come to understand is that if I *do* lose the job or relationship, it's because it's no longer right for me, and there's another better one waiting in the wings, so what's to be afraid of? We can be driven by fear thoughts or by abundance thoughts. Which do you prefer?

Use fear as a barometer that you are still growing. Through this perspective we begin to experience expectancy instead of anxiety. The word courage comes from the Latin word *cors*, meaning heart. Concentrate on breathing and take heart! Use the Celebration Strategies, breathe through the fear and you'll come out on the other side ready to take on more.

Affirmation: Today I will breathe through my fear.

Four

Sweet Surrender

At fifteen life had taught me undeniably that
surrender, in its place, was as honorable as
resistance, especially if one had no choice.
Maya Angelou

God alone knows the secret plan
Of the things he will do for the
world using my hand.
Toyohiko Kagawa

The word "surrender" can have such a positive meaning if we allow it. Giving up the "stuff" that creates stress in our lives can be a liberating experience. We can become accustomed to having worry, anxiety, old habits and material goods take up so much space in our everyday lives that life becomes just another thing to get through; a far cry from the celebration it could be. Letting go of these preconceptions and unhelpful habits can be difficult, but recognizing what is not working or what is stifling our ability to celebrate and then taking steps to let these hindrances go can be a worthwhile journey.

I think the hardest skill for me to learn
has been the skill of letting go.

In my search for contentment, I have had to let go of many things. My "cover," my willfulness, my plans, my idealism, my thoughts on how others "should" behave, my controlling behaviour, and even my escape fantasies. I have had to put away my mental running shoes and learn how to hang in.

Putting Up Walls

When I was 11 and living in a temporary foster home, my mother visited me one Sunday in September eager to share some good news. "I've been able to place you in Feller Institute" she said. "It's a co-ed boarding school in Grand Ligne Quebec. You'll love it there, I know you will." I was about to have an adventure!

I thought that maybe it would be different at a boarding school. I'd been staying in what felt like a holding tank since I'd come back from living with my dad. I'd read *The Secret Garden* by Frances Hodgson Burnett and had been longing for a best friend; maybe this would be my chance.

Nervous with anticipation, I got off the bus and had my first glimpse of Feller Institute. Tall gray stone buildings with small paned windows; black iron gates which swung open as I walked through them. I walked down the pebbled path and up to the big front door. I knocked, feeling nervous but hopeful, and I was ushered into the stark building. I would be in a bedroom with three other girls and although the building felt cold to me, I could hear the sound of laughter erupting from behind closed bedroom doors.

Once in my assigned room, I eagerly tore open a package my mother had given me and was so surprised by the pretty coral party dress that I hardly noticed there were bars on my window. Instead, I thought about the dances I'd wear my new dress to and the boys I'd be sure to meet. My pubescent hormones were already chirping; I knew I liked boys.

Soon the three other girls arrived. Two of them were sisters and spoke only in French. The third girl, Denise, had already been at Feller for a year. I liked her face and hoped we'd be friends. She had dark curly hair and was smaller than me. That year I'd grown three inches. Little bumps protruded from my chest, and my arms and legs felt too long for my body.

During the first week, one of my roommates smeared thick brown shoe polish all over my pretty coral party dress. That was no accident. I didn't tell anyone. I didn't want to cause any trouble.

School was the same old boring stuff. Teachers droning on, using pointers and snapping the strap if anyone giggled or spoke out of turn. All the kids wore gray woolen uniforms and white blouses or shirts. After class dismissal I watched as the boys disappeared quickly behind thick iron doors sealed with a large guillotine-like padlock. So much for my high hopes!

I began to feel lonely and scared. Denise already had a best friend, so after a few weeks I decided to leave Feller and get back to my mother. Every day I'd take something from the dining room, bread, fruit—anything not gooey—as preparation for my trip. I slit the lining of my coat and squirreled away my provisions and on Saturday morning, when the visitors were arriving, I walked right through them down the road, past the black gates and onto the street, which led to the highway. I stuck out my thumb and was quickly picked up. As soon as the driver found out where I came from, he promptly brought me back to Feller Institute. Of course I was punished. Six hours of solitary in a little green room with a tiny window overlooking a gray, stone wall.

Do you think that stopped me from running away again? Every Saturday, rain or shine, I ran away from boarding school. I don't know why the school authorities didn't just lock me up before-hand, but they didn't. I got to be an event! Older girls would throw candy and coins from the top floor, egging me on, placing bets on how far I'd get. Invariably the same thing happened: I'd make it through the gates, turn right at the corner, walk to the nearby highway, get picked up then returned to Feller Institute where the strap and that little green room awaited me.

One day a kindly bus driver took pity on me, brought me all the way to Montreal and let me off three blocks from my mother's apartment. I was so proud! I knew my mother would be happy to see me. After all, I'd managed to come over 100 miles by myself! She'd understand that I was a smart girl, a girl that could be helpful to her, and because of that she'd keep me with her. With great excitement I knocked on her door.

"What are you doing here?" my mother's face scowled when she saw me. She was not happy. After making a few phone calls, she took me down to the terminal and put me on the next bus back to Feller.

I never ran away again. I guess the school authorities figured it was because of the three days in solitary, but it was really because my heart felt broken. "My mother hates me, no one wants me, I'm glad I'm alone." I sort of liked solitary. At least it was private. Sitting on that little cot, biting my fingernails, and looking through the small window at the gray stone walls, I began to build walls of my own.

I built walls to protect me.

Walls of anger. Walls of defiance. Walls to keep me safe by keeping others distant. When I'd talk back in class and get the strap or have to sit in the wastebasket in front of everyone, it didn't matter. I could hide behind my walls and not feel a thing.

I used my walls as insulation

I used walls as insulation throughout my adolescence and right through my 20s. Gradually I began to understand that the very walls I'd erected to keep people out also kept me locked in. I'd built walls every bit as strong and thick as those steel walls that had separated the boys from the girls at Feller Institute! Finally I realized if I were ever going to get close to another human being, I'd have to surrender, admit defeat, acknowledge that I wasn't doing very well and start taking my walls down. I would have to do as Joanna Field advised: *Silence might be the privilege of the strong, but it was certainly a danger to the weak. For the things I was prompted to keep silent about were nearly always the things I was ashamed of, which would have been far better aired.*

My secrets kept me in enslaved, as did my feelings of shame and the belief that I was bad. Under my protective shield was the terrible pain of rejection I'd fended off so long ago. It was difficult allowing those feelings to surface, but they didn't last forever and the amazing truth I discovered was that when I let myself be vulnerable with people, even for a minute, good things happened. I didn't fall apart. In fact, the more I revealed about me, the more other people did the same. Then our connection would grow deeper and we'd become closer. The more that happened, the easier it became to self-disclose and the freer I felt. I wanted more of that freedom, so I opened my heart and my mouth and just kept on opening.

Letting Go

In the past I equated being brave with being stoic, which meant keeping silent about what bothered me and maintaining a stiff upper lip. Today I'm not as outwardly brave as I once appeared to be. Today my greatest acts of courage are talking about how I genuinely feel or asking for help when I need it, without ducking for cover or using anger to hide behind. Slowly,

I've learned to surrender.

To accept life on life's terms, and take others as they are. And still it is difficult to do, even though I know the reality of surrendering is so sweet, and leads to a quiet inner peace. But oh, the struggle to get there! Some of us are hard-headed, and we need to have "letting go lessons" come at us again and again until we get the message.

I got one of those messages when I was working for three months at a holistic health center. My job was cleaning and chopping vegetables and I hated it. Every day I waged war within myself, gritting my teeth, telling myself that in five or six more hours the day would be over. The thing was, I loved the perks that went with the job; living in community, having my food and dishes done for me, going to spiritual gatherings, taking yoga classes. I knew the work was a small price to pay for the goodies that came with it.

One morning I was sitting outside on my mid-morning break, muttering to myself about how other people spent more time talking than chopping and how I worked harder than anyone else when suddenly a big wind gusted all around me and someone's bike helmet hit me squarely on the head. Ouch! My head throbbed. I sat there dazed, and at the same time amazed, because in that instant I saw that I was wasting my time thinking about how bad my lot was. What I had to do instead was concentrate on the good, on the gifts I was getting. Miraculously, the wind died right down, I picked up the helmet, placed it on the bike and went back to work determined to find ways I could *enjoy* peeling carrots, chopping onions and dicing celery. I thought of how people would receive benefit from eating my well-prepared vegetables and concentrated on finding joy in each chop and dice.

Many times since I have called on that lesson. Whenever I notice my internal whine beginning, I reach for a positive thought. I ask myself whether I am contributing to the problem or the solution. I remind myself that I am in the right place getting whatever lesson I need to be getting. In other words, I surrender. To whom? And to what? To something larger than myself. Something greater than my ego.

The bliss of surrender comes through doing it.

It doesn't really matter what we surrender to, as long as it is not one person, because that becomes co-dependency and creates another set of problems. We can surrender to the ceiling or the sky, to the stars, the moon, to nature, to a force beyond us, to an energy, or to a higher power. To surrender we need to believe that *there is something greater than ourselves,* or we won't let go of our ego.

We can surrender to our notion of God. For some of us this is difficult. *Very* difficult. Relying on God, however we understand God's presence, is foreign to many of us. We've been encouraged from early childhood to be self-reliant. Even when we desperately need help, we fear asking for it. It used to be that way for me, especially trusting in GOD (which, if need be, can stand for Good Orderly Direction). The important thing is to do it. Stop holding your breath, exhale and trust.

When I was little, I thought God was a big white-bearded man who sat on a giant throne in heaven and kept score of all the wrong things you did, and then punished you for your sins by sending you to hell, which was a fiery inferno. What a scary picture. I tried believing. I prayed that I would be kept safe and I wasn't, that my family be brought back to me, and it didn't happen, so I gave up on God and lived life on my terms.

Those were the years I thought I had to do it all myself; take responsibility for everything, run the show, stall any disasters. It was hard holding up the sky, making sure others did it "right." And as you may have gathered, I was self-righteous and opinionated too, convinced I had *the* answers. I kept a mental grudge list of all the people I believed had wronged me, starting with my mother. I wasn't keen on forgiveness either.

My life didn't become a cause for celebration until I acknowledged that doing it *my way* just didn't work. For Frank Sinatra it might have, but not for me. That was my first step toward creating heaven on earth. You see, in thinking I had to do it all by myself *I was playing God!* Like a mad conductor, trying to get the orchestra (everyone else) in tune, I was frantically scurrying about, denying or covering up my mistakes, pretending to be perfect, insisting that others follow my lead, living with enormous guilt and shame, wailing about my lot in life, then feeling contrite. Endlessly cycling in that pattern, stuck on a circling merry-go-round, unable to get off.

Listen to What's There

How did I make the big switch? I arrived at a place in my life where I felt defeated. Oh, I had material things: a house, a job, three kids and two cats. But I was hollow inside, sick with a spiritual deadness. I knew I'd lost "it," what ever the "it" was. I felt empty. Life was going by me but I was not "in it." I felt as though I was a goldfish flopping outside a glass bowl, watching other fish swimming happily about, knowing I wasn't even in the water. Can you identify with any of this?

I gave up playing God and accepted a Higher Power whom I chose to call God, even though I didn't trust him/her/it. Nonetheless, I acted "as if." I spoke to this God, asking for direction, never thinking I'd get any. One day I began to hear a little voice inside of me, gently nudging me. I trusted this voice because intuitively I knew it was leading me towards an important discovery—myself. Soon I began to hear wisdom from friends—even strangers—and sensed that there was a loving presence speaking to me through them. Bit by bit I started to trust that there was some benevolent force guiding my life. It became apparent that the more I surrendered my willfulness and asked for direction, the more I was guided to do exactly what it was I needed to do. I did this with my entire life, including career and relationships. First I handed over my career aspirations in the form of a prayer. It went something like this:

Dear God. You know I want to give seminars and speak because it's my passion and I believe I have something of value to offer people, something that will help them. If you want me to do this work, please send it to me, and if it is not your will, please show me what else you want me to do.

That was it. I said my prayer in the mornings and soon the work came. I never did market my services in the conventional sense because I trusted God to be my marketer. Some of my colleagues tease me about this unconventional form of marketing, but they can't argue with success.

Trust the Cycles

Of course, I have to do the legwork: the planning, preparation and delivery of my presentations. But I go where I am led. There are times when I have little income and I still say the same prayer. If the work doesn't come, it's usually because I have other issues to attend to, or need to take a break. I trust the cycles. No longer do I make a five-year plan because I know my life is in the hands of the master planner.

I did the same thing with my love life. I asked my Higher Power to send me someone whom I could love and be loved by *if it was right for me*, and my partner arrived shortly after the request. I believe this happened because I was willing to accept what was placed in front of me. I can tell you that my husband is kind, loving, thoughtful, considerate, not rich and not tall. He is exactly what I need, but not what I thought I wanted. I'm happier than I've ever been, so something must be working.

Do I live my life in bliss? Much of the time yes, I do. And then there are those days. Like that day last August. That day last August I had a plan. I was at our cottage for a couple of weeks enjoying precious alone time. I had an agenda. I would get up early, and write for three hours no matter what. No phone calls, no disturbances. I had a plan!

Cutting out my morning yoga and meditation ritual, I opened the laptop and discovered it was frozen. Not one command would it register. I tried hitting every key, nothing happened. Tried unplugging it, jiggling it, shaking it around, jabbing the keys, speaking nicely, swearing at it. Nothing worked. Off to the Yellow Pages, searching for service. "Bring it in by noon. You're lucky, our service man is in today." I packed up the computer and jumped into the car. As I brushed a strand of hair out of my eyes, a piercing sting struck my hand and a wasp flew out of my hair. OUCH! Immediately my hand started swelling. That was a clue for me to slow down, to stop for a breather. However, because I had a plan, I didn't stop. Stomping back to the cottage, I put some ice in a cloth, bound my hand, and started the 20-minute trip to the nearest town. Halfway there I got a flat tire.

I located a garage and two hours later arrived at the computer store. It was now almost noon. I got the thing fixed and bought a cartridge for the printer, which I suspected, was out of ink. Then I drove home, put the cartridge in the printer only to discover it was the wrong size.

I let out few three-second screams[1] and finally the computer started. Simultaneously, the left lens popped out of my eyeglasses, the little pin holding the frame together made a tiny pinging sound, then slipped through a crack in the floorboards, lost forever.

---

1 This is a strategy I discuss in my previous book, _Celebrating Anger—Creative Solutions for Managing Conflict at Home, on the Job, and in Relationships_ (Toronto: Performance Plus Publishing, 1993, 1999), at p. 26. In a chapter called "Instant Interventions" I suggest cupping hands around the mouth and letting go with a few screams whenever we get frustrated. No one knows what we're doing and we get rid of tension in a way that won't harm us or others.

I can't write without my glasses. So there I was. Knowing I had to let go and surrender. Obviously, nothing was going to work until I did. Picking up a towel, I meandered down to the river, plunged in and swam off my frustration. Then I sat on the dock and dangled my feet in the water, soaking up the sun and listening to the birds. After an hour or so I went back, taped my eyeglasses together and began writing. It was now 5 P.M. I felt relaxed and the writing came easily. When I next looked up, three hours had flown by.

Later, when reviewing my day, I realized I'd forgotten to surrender it. And yes, there have been plenty of occasions when I've had an agenda or have been caught up in someone else's, when I knew I had to take time out and quiet myself but didn't. I pay for these times by getting more stressed and less accomplished. Conversely, when I do let go, when I release my agenda and open myself to being in the moment, invariably I find there is a gift waiting for me. I learn something new, or discover I can be of help to someone else.

Now my intention is to live in surrender mode. To make my plans, but let the outcome be what my Higher Power has in mind. To relinquish my willfulness, cultivate that small voice within and do what is in front of me to the best of my ability. Breathe and remember that interruptions can be angels bearing gifts. Deal with challenges. Give thanks at the end of the day and be grateful for whatever comes my way. Live life on life's terms. I used to think that if I let go it would be a recipe for chaos. In fact, it's just the opposite.

The miracle in letting go is that every time we do, everything works better.

When I am distressed, just by sitting quietly for a while I become peaceful. Then I can hear the inner nudge and follow instructions or make a phone call to a friend and ask for input. All

I have to do is ask for help in order to have it. It works 100% of the time. With odds like these, why gamble?

The sweetness of surrender and the value of listening to inner wisdom were lessons I learned one summer weekend. My brother and his partner were arriving from England after a brief sojourn in Montreal. They were slated to arrive Friday evening. My two oldest and dearest friends were also scheduled to come for the weekend. It would be a bit cramped but I figured we could manage. The friends would be arriving at about 1 P.M. Friday. I had a last minute clean-up to do and told myself I should do it in the morning but I wrote instead.

At noon I started the clean-up. Two hours later it was finished. I was frazzled and needed a walk. Should I go or not? I wanted to greet my friends after their six-hour drive and they'd be arriving any moment. At the same time I knew I needed to get out and breathe some air, exercise my body and replenish my spirit, so I opted for the walk. Forty minutes later I came back, refreshed and expectant, and within five minutes my dear friends arrived. Three hours after their appointed time, but right on divine time.

Delighted to see them, I felt completely available because I had taken care of my own needs instead of martyring myself to "I must clean up first and make sure everything looks spic and span for them and I must be there smiling as they arrive." That's the way I used to live; thankfully I don't fall into that trap as much now.

We were catching up on family news, when my husband called from the city to say his car wasn't ready. He'd taken the car to a mechanic for a repair and the part needed wouldn't arrive until Saturday morning. He wouldn't leave for the cottage until then. As I listened to his story, I became more and more agitated because every Friday night for the previous seven weeks he had said he was coming up to the cottage and, without exception, something had happened to delay his arrival until Saturday noon. I had a sneaking suspicion that these delays were symptomatic of his desire to stay home on Friday night and hang out alone. Why didn't he just tell me that?

Taking a deep breath and remembering to exhale just as deeply, I asked him to be honest and look beyond the situations he created to keep him in the city. "Be fair to me, so I don't feel set-up and subsequently disappointed when you don't arrive." I explained. This was a far cry from my habitual response, which was to complain or blame. I felt calm and relaxed when I got off the phone.

My friends and I had a lovely evening, reminiscing and sharing experiences. We have been friends throughout my previous marriages, and having time to just talk freely without explaining details was a luxury. In the morning we drove to the farmer's market and when we came back, my husband was waiting, eager to be with us. Meanwhile, no word from my brother. Nothing to do but let go of that one.

I turned on the answering machine and went for a canoe ride. Later that afternoon my brother called, explaining how he'd tried to rent a car in Montreal, but hadn't brought his licence, so that plan was out. I gave him bus information and sure enough there was a bus he could catch that would get him within a couple of hours of our cottage late Sunday afternoon. This gave us a full day to enjoy our friends who were scheduled to return home Sunday evening. Then another little miracle occurred. The appointment for which my friends had been going back to the city got postponed to late Monday afternoon, giving them time to stay and visit with my brother, whom they hadn't seen in many years.

We all had a wonderful evening playing games and laughing boisterously. Once my husband and friends left, my brother and his partner and I had a few days to spend together. It all worked out beautifully, albeit not according to plan.

Letting Go is Never Easy

Although letting go can be difficult, the good news is the rewards are greater than the task.

My cat Toby helps me remember to surrender. When Toby snuggles in my arms at night, I feel his little body relax in stages, and I try to follow his example. His letting go reminds me to do the same. Maybe life is just one big experience of surrendering.

I'm learning how to surrender my attachment to material things, particularly clothes and books. My closet is full of outfits I've been hanging onto for more than 10 years. I like them all, but I don't wear them all. I *believe* that if I don't wear something for more than a year, it needs to go, but do I live what I believe? No, I hold on. I'm afraid that if I let go I won't have enough. I know this fear comes from childhood deprivation, however, I haven't been a child for a long time, so why do I still hang onto the belief *and* the clothes?

Twenty years ago I went on a year-long trip to Europe. Needing to rent my house out, I had to scale down, so I got rid of a lot of "stuff." It left me feeling light and free. I enjoyed traveling with only a knapsack and even managed to shed some of what I carried on my back. For most of that year I maintained a simple lifestyle, and loved it. About a month before I returned, I started accumulating gifts for friends and mementos for me. I had to lug my purchases with me, so I bought a suitcase, then another. By the time I returned I was feeling overloaded. In the past 20 years I've managed to gather as much as I once got rid of. What I need to do now is deal with my fear and clear out clutter by giving stuff away. It is time to have another pack-up-and-give-to-Goodwill purge.

The Radiance of Surrender

Have you noticed that people who live a surrendered life seem to have a radiance about them, an aura like those halos artists have made visible around the heads of saints? I remember seeing a shimmering light around the head of Richard Moss, one of my spiritual teachers. He lived with few possessions, and treasured people. Mother Teresa has been described as being "full of light." Malcolm Muggeridge wrote: "Something of God's universal love rubbed off on Mother Teresa, giving her homely features a noticeable luminosity, a shining quality." I think we bring more light into our lives when we surrender. We leave space for a higher energy to fill us up with love. Love is the inner radiance and people are automatically attracted to it.

Sophie Burnham, in her illuminating book *The Ecstatic Journey* describes her experience of surrendering:[2]

> *I surrendered with my last coherent thoughts . . . I said. . . .*
> *I belong only to God. . . . With that I was immersed in a sweetness words can not express. Wave after wave of light washed over me. But this is wrong, because I was the light as well. . . .*
> *When I looked down I saw light streaming off the palms of my hands. I could feel it pulsating off my palms in waves, I could see it flaring, flashing in everything; the fields were shining with light. And so were the people gathering at the hotel, talking to one another and shining with their inner light.*

With eyes to see and love to feel, our world is transformed and we are never the same again. When we surrender we walk in the light and the light emanates out from us. The following Celebration Strategies provide some suggestions for surrendering.

---

2 *The Ecstatic Journey* (New York: The Ballantine Publishing Group, New York, 1997), at p. 80.

Celebration Strategies

1. When you find yourself becoming agitated or stressed, S.T.O.P!

Use the word **STOP** as an acronym for coming back into balance. Train your mind to think of the word **STOP** whenever you are stressed.

S stands for **S**tressed

T for **T**ired

O for **O**verwhelmed

P means: **P**ut everything on hold.

Just **STOP!**

2. Concentrate on breathing deeply and slowly.

Breathe from your belly all the way up through your chest. Relax your shoulders, relax your jaw and simply breathe deeply. Exhale fully. Do this at least three times. Then stand up, stretch, walk around, swing your arms back and forth, roll your shoulders forward and back a few times, get yourself a glass of water and resume your task.

3. Discover your own higher power.

It can be anything you want it to be. If you don't believe, fake it and trust the process.

4. Visualize yourself giving whatever worry, anxiety, fear or burdens you have to your higher power.

Release your troubles. Let them go. Feel the lightness, the ease in your shoulders. Know that all is well.

5. **Give your day to your higher power early in the morning, asking to be shown what you can do all through the day.**
End by giving thanks at night before you go to bed.

6. **Breathe light, goodness and love into your body.**
Exhale willfulness, resentment and expectations. Repeat this process three or four times a day.

7. **Clear out accumulated clutter.**
Give it to friends, have a garage sale or send it to your favourite charity. Let go of all the "stuff" that weighs you down so you can travel lightly.

When we are surrender we are always on vacation.

Affirmation: I am willing to let go. I am serene and content.

Five

Tame the Inner Tigers

You cannot create a statue by smashing the
marble with a hammer, and you cannot
by force of arms release the spirit
or the soul of man.
Confucius

Don't see the other human being angrily,
see your own anger!
Evagrius Ponticus

First, keep peace within yourself, then you
can bring peace to others.
Thomas à Kempis

We all have inner tigers. Those raging insatiable beasts that spring out of nowhere and claw into our lives, tearing our peace to shreds, biting into other people. Then just as quickly they become satiated, bid a hasty retreat and vanish again—for a while. This chapter is about identifying those tigers and taming them so we won't be victims of ourselves.

> *Tyger, Tyger burning bright in the forests of the night,*
> *What beloved hand or eye could frame thy*
> *fearful symmetry?*
> William Blake

I've always loved these lines, visualizing the tiger taut, waiting to pounce, energy momentarily contained, yet coiled, ready to spring out at any moment—passionate and purposeful. Passion is a subject poets write reams about, but what about its kissing cousin: anger? You don't find poems praising rage, eulogizing an "Ode to His Angry Nature" or a "Sonnet to Her Vengeful Spewing." Passion we like; anger—that's another story. Who wants to admit we have anger? Who wants to confess to dumping anger on others, randomly assigning blame, sulking with silent scorn and infecting themselves with resentments? Yet, we all do. If we don't acknowledge our anger, we're shortchanging ourselves. When we shut down our anger, we lock up our passion as well. The good news is that anger can help us really get to know ourselves. Used wisely, it can be a tool for transformation. The bad news is that if we don't change our habits, we will become a casualty—of ourselves

When I turned 13, my saga of living at foster homes finally ended. My mother located a three-bedroom apartment, found a roomer to help pay the rent, and brought me to live with her. It was a new beginning. A month later, I got a surprise telephone call from my dad. I hadn't heard from him in two years. "Princess, what I want you to do is go to the liquor store and buy me a bottle of Alcool. Then, bring it to the Montreal General Hospital quick as you can. This is my medicine, and I need it. Will you do that for me?"

Stealthily, I snuck my hand into my mother's purse and was almost out the door when she caught me.

"What have you got in your hand?" She pried open my fingers, watching the dollar bills fly to the floor. "Get to your room, you bad girl!"

"But I need this money. It's for Daddy. I have to buy him some medicine."

"There's nothing you can do for Daddy. Now, get to your room, you sneak thief."

The next evening, my mother got a phone call. Slowly, she put down the receiver, went to the bathroom and very deliberately brushed her teeth. I knew something was wrong.

"What is it? What's happened? Please tell me!"

"Your father is dead," she replied in a flat voice. "He died at the hospital this afternoon from cirrhosis of the liver."

"No, that's not true. It's can't be true. It's all your fault. You should have let me get him his medicine!" I yelled at her hysterically.

"You're lucky I stopped you. He'd bribed an orderly to bring him a bottle and that's what killed him." She retorted.

My Dad was dead at 43. It took me years to understand that my mother had saved me from administering the final blow to my father. She had kept me safe by banishing me to my room that fateful night. But at the time I blamed her and wished it were she who was in the casket.

After my father died, I felt my own dreams were over. Life became something to get out of. Like the hero from *A Stone for Danny Fisher*, the Harold Robbins novel I was reading—I wanted to "live fast, die young and leave a good-looking corpse." My intention was to cram all my living into a short period of time and be dead before I was 30. So I went chasing after excitement.

Throughout those teenaged years, when any man paid me attention, I thought it was love and it meant I had some worth.

When a child does not feel valued,
she doesn't know who or what to value.

I rode with bikers and discovered booze, which gave me courage and made me feel daring. Intermittently, I also went out with college boys and went to proms, for which my mother scrimped and made me pretty party dresses. I felt uncomfortable in those dresses, as if I was playing a role. I knew the truth; I was bad and full of shame. I didn't deserve nice dresses, or clean, smart boys. At one of those dances I was re-introduced to Scotty Gormley, my childhood friend. It quickly became apparent that we had nothing in common. We lived in different worlds.

My mother saved up and bought me a membership at a prestigious club where she and my father had once belonged. She wanted me to meet a "good caliber of people." I reacted by bringing my black boyfriend, running up a bar chit, and cashing in on shock value. I tuned out at school and pretended I was fine, but I had to use props to do it. Books were my first means of escape, then came movies, television, sugar, cigarettes, alcohol, pills, boys, men and finally, work. These were the substances I used to avoid being with myself, to avoid feeling the sadness and pain I'd run away from.

Deep down, there were tigers roaming in the jungle of my emotions. I knew there was something wrong. A beast was raging within me, gathering momentum. I fought incessantly with my mother, blaming her for everything. At 16 I left home and moved into the YWCA.

I worked as a typist in an advertising agency, but soon tired of that, so I went back to school at night and continued my education. In my early 20s, I got married and subsequently had three children. In my 30s I got divorced, re-married, then divorced again. I drank away my troubles, became bleary-eyed, sadder and—eventually—suicidal. Finally, I came to what felt like a dead end. The road I was traveling on was leading to destruction. I could see that I was playing chicken with my life, driving too speedily, racing ever faster just to keep my terror at bay.

During a weekend trip to New York, another road beckoned to me. I'd gone with a girlfriend who also liked to drink and party. The first night we were there, a telephone number popped into my head—the number of a friend I hadn't seen in years. When we met,

I noticed she wasn't drinking. She told me she'd stopped seven years earlier, and had been going to a self-help program since that time. In a flash of recognition, I realized I too had a problem.

My friend took me to a meeting where I saw happy people with sparkling eyes—people who reached out and helped each other. I had a choice to make. Would I continue on my reckless path or turn towards this path of hope? Would I slow down or keep running? Would I begin to examine myself and my life or call it all a crock and continue to nurture resentments? Hesitantly, full of fear, I stepped onto a new path.

First, I had to give up drinking and taking pills. Self-destruction had to stop. By joining a 12-step program, I was able to let go of the anesthetics I had used to numb myself. Next, I had to unravel the cocoon I'd been hiding in and face the light of day. This meant I had to acknowledge the anger that stormed inside me and understand that, although it had protected me for a time, it now kept me hostage. Beneath my anger lived my pain; all the sorrow I'd stored up and never dealt with. It was time to grieve my losses; time to accept that I would never be able to go back and do my childhood over. There was no magic wand to wave, no elixir to make it better. There would be no reconciliation, no family restored.

What a painful awareness! I couldn't take it in all at once. Sometimes I'd be driving and would start crying for no apparent reason. Other times, I'd hear a certain strain of music and feel unbearably sad. Sunday afternoons were terrible, until I realized I was waiting to be abandoned again. Bit by bit, I leaked out my sorrow, privately, one tear at a time. I'd been emotionally frozen; it was a slow thaw.

When I finally understood, at a gut level, that I could not change the past, I was able to begin accepting that what had happened in my childhood had actually happened and was now over. The nightmare was done and I could awake. Through feeling my pain I could release some shame, let go of my bravado and start to heal. This became my game plan: to do whatever I needed to do to heal. And, when I'd done my own healing, I'd help others do the same. I resolved to focus on helping people deal with anger, because it had been such a strong force in my life. It became my passion and my life's work.

When we repress anger, we can develop unhealthy behaviours and become seriously ill. If we express anger carelessly, we hurt others who also get sick—of *us*! For many of us, anger is like a lit cigarette. There's some smoke, some fire and you can see it smoldering. But when we throw the cigarette into the woods, it can become a raging fire, out of control. We need to be careful where we throw our anger. If, on the other hand, we keep on shelving our resentments, they still burn brightly inside of us and eventually we will become sick.

Clearly, we need an alternative. We could sit down and have an honest look at our relationship with anger. Then make a truce with it.

I had no idea there was another option.

For many years I was stuck in reactive mode. You know what that's like: someone says or does something, and we react with a knee-jerk response. Here's an example. You criticize me, I rise to the bait, and either defend myself or attack you back. I had no idea there was any another option—like watching or listening when one of my buttons was pushed. Watching without doing anything, simply noticing my instinctive response and my desire to strike back—noticing, but not doing. Today I am happy to report there are times I can actually do this, even when I'm triggered.

Recently, a friend blasted me for not returning her calls. I wanted to tell her that I had struggles of my own, like too much to do and too little time. I wanted to exonerate myself and push back at her and, while I was mentally preparing my comeback, I saw another choice. I could say nothing. I could let my friend vent, feel my own discomfort, release my defensive shoulders, breathe, and say nothing. I could practise patience. So that's what I did. I concentrated on breathing instead of reacting. Guess what happened? She said her piece, calmed down and started chatting about something else. I didn't get snagged. There had been no harsh words, no remorse or guilt to churn around later. What a payoff!

The Best Defence Might Be No Defence

Father Abbott, a desert monk said, "Any trial that comes to you whatsoever can be conquered by silence." That's sage advice, as long as we are not using silence to punish. Have you ever done that—used silence as a weapon, to manipulate or get back at someone? I've tried, for about half an hour. That's as long as I can last before anxiety gets hold of me, and I usually end up blurting out my anger and later, regretting it. My mother used silence, often to her advantage. I, however, was on the receiving end, drowning in anxiety. Not good. I don't think this is what Father Abbott intended. I suspect he was advising us to use silence for ourselves, to grow through our discomforts. Used that way, silence *is* golden.

My friend Lorraine and I once had the following conversation about the legal wranglings of her separation and divorce.

Lorraine: "I've gone to a lawyer, and he agrees. I should be compensated for leaving the city and moving to be with Glenn. He figures I can get at least half of Glenn's house as well in the settlement."

For some reason, my buttons were getting pushed when she said she was suing Glenn for half his property, so I said something like:

"If Fraser and I split up, and he went after my condo, which I worked hard to buy long before I met him, I'd fight him all the way. I think it's fair to divide whatever you've accumulated in the time you've been together, and maybe you have compensation due, although as I recall, he's financially supported you, and it was your choice to move to his town just as it's your choice to leave now. However, I don't think you have the right to go after the property he bought before you ever came on the scene."

There was silence on the other end. Clearly, I was identifying with Glenn and offering input that Lorraine had not asked for. She reacted by telling me she didn't want to continue our conversation and hung up the phone. And I, thinking I was right and morally superior, had come face-to-face with my unsolicited advice giving, and self-right-eousness. The adage, "You're never angry for the reason you think," flickered through my brain, dancing like sunlight around the gray matter. I let go with a few three-second screams, then asked myself why I was so upset. What was really going on with me?

Only by taking the time to ask myself what was really going on would I get to the truth.

I spent some time gnawing on the question bone, and came up with what seemed a reasonable answer—my sense of justice was offended, my belief in fair play challenged. That's what it was—or was it? As I am prone to rationalization, I probed further and ran smack into my own guilt.

When I decided I no longer wanted to be in relationship with my first husband, I went to a lawyer and got a restraining order, forbidding him to enter our home. My mother had given me the down payment for that house bought four years earlier, and the house was in my name, so I kept it. Then I replaced my husband with the young man I was seeing. Later I moaned about the miserable pittance of child support my ex-husband contributed, but I never really looked at me, at my actions, at how I appro-priated the house!

Lorraine's words had triggered my defense mechanism. I'd wanted to keep my behaviour hidden from my own eyes so I wouldn't have to see me as I was. As long as I could project upon her, I wouldn't have to look at what I'd done. I'd been greedy and self-centered, living from a sense of entitlement. Only by taking the time to ask myself what was really going on, did I get to the truth.

I knew I had to call Lorraine back and tell her what I'd discovered, apologize for moralizing and make some amends. I also had the option of apologizing to my ex-husband. I have done this before, now I think it serves a better purpose to make sure I don't discredit him in any conversations with our grown children—especially when they serve him up to me as bait. I picked up the phone, and dialed Lorraine's number.

My Teachers

People who push my buttons are important teachers!

I have learned, reluctantly, that if I react with anger to something someone says or does, it's invariably because I'm hiding something from myself. I've come to value people who push my buttons as important teachers, because they shed light on those areas of darkness. When I get mad at something someone else does or says, it's a first rate opportunity to look at me. I've learned to take advantage of the situation, because often the other person is simply mirroring one of my own habits or characteristics; probably the very one I am most in denial about.

None of us like to think of ourselves as flawed. We like to pretend we've got it together and, like Mary Poppins, we're practically perfect. When someone does or says something we don't like and we react with anger, it is usually because we do the very same thing, but pretend to ourselves that we don't. We use anger as a defense to ward off the truth.

People who activate us are our professors, and guess what? They're usually found in our immediate families. I'll share a case in point. I have a good relationship with both of my daughters. I can also get activated by them, as they can by me.

My youngest daughter came to stay with me last summer, after spending several years living on her own. Not surprisingly, we had power struggles and control issues. I found myself falling into the trap of reacting to what she said with anger, then feeling self-pity because I thought she was disrespectful. Finally, I saw that

my reaction was my responsibility

and I could exercise some restraint. The next time she lashed out at me I said nothing. I just walked away, and let the space hang. I didn't rush in to make it better and, at the same time, I didn't punish her with stony silence. I kept the conversation light.

You know what happened? She acknowledged that she had been wrong to yell at me. We hugged and talked about our difficulties. I could hear how my attempts at scheduling activities annoyed her and resolved to stop doing it. She understood that her dropping articles of clothing on every available chair irritated me. We made some ground rules then went for a walk. It was a good outcome because I wasn't reactive. The neat thing is, it takes only one person to change the game (preferably the one reading this book.)

Healing Opportunities

In those rare cases where I am absolutely certain the person I am mad at is not mirroring something that I do, then it's usually an area I need to do more healing work on.

My partner, Fraser, is a smoker. During the past 12 years, he has made many attempts to quit; at least one a year. He becomes bad tempered, I react, we start fighting and he smokes again. I'm a reformed smoker and I really want Fraser to be smoke-free. Both his parents died from lung cancer, so the odds are not in his favour. I nag. He stops—for a while. Have you ever tried to change someone? Has it worked?

The last time Fraser stopped was different. Resolving not to get caught in the same trap, I became the model wife—solicitous, sympathetic, understanding and supportive of him, patient beyond belief, tolerating his moods, welcoming his anger, hanging in through the withdrawal grumpiness, assuring him that this too would pass. Then, I got a call from a client wanting me to travel to Western Canada and give their folks my conflict management seminar. I leapt at the opportunity. For three weeks I was on the road, and by the end of the tour, I felt tired but gratified. The participants had been elated with the program, and I felt proud and happy.

Riding up the escalator at Toronto International Airport, I was serene and eager to see my sweetheart. And there he was, waiting at the gate, flowers in hand. "What a lovely man," I thought. We merged together in a clinch, and then I felt it—that oh-so-familiar square cigarette box pressing against my hip.

My inner voice of consciousness kicked in, telling me to back off. I took one step, opened my mouth and said, "How could you do this to me? You promised me you wouldn't smoke. I believed you! You broke your promise. Obviously, I can't trust you. God knows what else you were doing while I was away. I can't live with someone I can't trust." Then I threw the flowers on the ground and stormed off, only to realize that I had no car and no money. Turning around, sheepishly I asked for a ride home.

Fraser gave me a steely look and picked up my bags. During the silent ride home I thought about what I'd said and done. In one moment I'd tipped from radiant happiness to accusatory dementia. Obviously, I'd been triggered, but why? Using my own formula, I decided to investigate. Do I break promises? I try very hard not to break them to others, but yes, I break promises to myself. Last January, I promised myself I'd write every day and I didn't even start until July. And there's more. I've broken promises to my children, told them they could have things, then later recanted. I'm not proud of this, but I tell you because it's the truth. I do the very thing I accused him of. Gulp.

Quietness hung heavy during our long drive home. Arriving at our apartment, I turned towards Fraser, wanting to make up. The set of his jaw showed me this was not a good time. I followed him up the stairs, sat down on the couch and asked myself another question: *"Did someone break promises to me when I was little?"* In a flash, it all came back. I could see my father as he tiptoed quietly into my room that night in Peterborough, reaching into the closet and taking down the old brown suitcase.

"Where are you going, Daddy?"

"Oh, nowhere sweetheart. I'm just going to clean this old thing out. We'll go fishing tomorrow, I promise."

In the morning, my dad and the suitcase were gone. I waited and waited for him to come back, but he never did. It tore my heart to shreds, because I loved my father more than anyone in the world. I spent years waiting for him to return, even after he was dead—waiting, interminably, for Daddy to return.

Now, I'm all grown up. I've had therapy. I even give therapy to others. I know about the disease of alcoholism and promises broken. I know my father was not a bad man, just a sick one. I've worked hard on healing my past, but there are still times I get activated, and those cigarettes in Fraser's pocket were a prime example. What was really going on in me was that I was afraid I would lose Fraser, just like I lost my father.

Since working with anger for more than two decades, I've learned that both fear and pain reside beneath anger.

We need to find an opportunity for healing.

The antidote is to feel the feelings, and they will pass. I sat on the couch for a few moments, feeling the sadness that my younger self had experienced waiting for her dad. Then I gently approached Fraser, who was still stony faced.

"Fraser, my sweetheart, please come and sit down beside me," I motioned to the couch. Sitting side-by-side is a conflict management technique we practise. It is not confrontational, and it keeps us physically on the same side, like a team. Reaching for his hand, I began telling him what I'd discovered. I told him about my father, and why I react to broken promises. Told him about my fears. "I love you and don't want you to die from smoking." I blubbered. "I don't want to lose you."

Smiling, he responded, "I love you too, and I miss you when you're traveling. That's why I started smoking. I'll quit again. I promise."

Well, maybe he will and maybe he won't. It's not my business. What I need to do is let Fraser be and work with my own issues. My job is to de-activate my inner bombs. The cigarette episode was a valuable learning experience because I was able to see that I did break my own promises and that I needed more healing around loss.

Every time I do some inner work, I think it's finished forever and it's always a surprise when I discover there's still more to do. I think life moves us in circular patterns. The old stuff gets activated again on a deeper level. We release more and become a bit freer each time it comes up. Doing anger work is like peeling an endless onion.

As long as we're breathing, there's more to work on.

When life angers us, when that onion stings or makes us cry, it's a good sign. It lets us know that we're still alive, and we have more growing to do. We can get immediate release by yelling for three seconds, or by writing a rage letter, or venting with a friend. Then, we can look behind our anger and see what's waiting.

Identifying Triggers

We're never angry for the reason we think.

Anger is like a mask; it covers up feelings of guilt, shame or pain: feelings we'd rather not experience. So, the next time you get triggered, take off the mask and see what's behind it.

Jerry, a client, was laid off from his job. When we spoke, he was still in shock.

"I can't believe it. I've worked for X Company for 28 years, and then they gave me notice that I had to be out in 24 hours. I couldn't see it coming, either. Sure, I got a package, but that's not the point. It's how they handled it that bothers me—like I'm a nothing, a no-body. After 28 years, all I got was 'Get out'."

Jerry spent three months sitting at home alone, watching television all day, feeling helpless and becoming more depressed.

People tend to feel helpless when they think they're trapped, or backed into a corner from which there is no escape. That is an illusion! There is always a way out.

It's by going through that we get out.

Jerry realized that he had to deal with his depression. It was immobilizing him. That's when he came to see me. My job was to help him access his underlying feelings and deal with the shame he'd been denying. Jerry felt like he'd failed, or worse, *that he was a failure.* When he traced that feeling back to a childhood experience, he was able to process and let it go. He learned that the past does not equal the future. Shame is a feeling and not a fact. Once Jerry was able to express his feelings, he could access more energy. He moved quickly into recovery mode. He started exercising and spent time asking himself what he wanted to do with the rest of his life.

The past does not equal the future.

When I last saw him, there were not enough hours in the day for Jerry. With his severance money, he had opened a bicycle shop—a lifelong dream. He was taking a photography class, had bought himself a puppy, and was helping other men who'd been laid off. He had energy and enthusiasm to spare!

Dealing with Depression

Depression is often anger with the stinger turned inwards. It can be a useful signal, letting us know that we need to process our feelings. I'm not talking about chronic depression here, for that needs medical attention, but just the ordinary garden variety of feeling down, losing energy, or having a diminished sense of esteem. There are many drugs available to deal with clinical depression, and that's a good thing. But, even when even drugs are indicated, we still need to identify the cause, feel the feelings, and deal with it.

To relieve minor depression, get out your pen and paper and ask yourself: *What am I depressed or sad about?* Trust your inner wisdom. Keep asking yourself the question, and write whatever comes until you have nothing more to say.

Then ask: *How can I deal with this feeling?* Realize you have options. You could have a cleansing cry; you could talk to a friend, write about it in your journal, and see a doctor or a therapist. Later, you could get some exercise, go for a walk, clean out some clutter, watch a funny movie, do some gardening or start a new project.

Listen to your inner answer and take action. The moment we take action on our own behalf, our depression lifts.

Are you Mount Vesuvius?

Perhaps you are like Mount Vesuvius—the exploding type who blames and dumps anger on others, then feels justified, at least for a while. Susan was like that.

"I didn't know how to stop. I'd do the same thing over and over. At work, I was busy but in control. The moment I got home, I'd scream at the kids and fight with my husband. Every time I yelled, I'd feel badly afterwards, but those mean words just seemed to erupt from me. Sometimes, I smacked my son. I know this was wrong, but I couldn't seem to do anything else."

Susan was in trouble. Her inner tiger had to get tamed. For starters, she needed to manage her stress by learning how to breathe deeply and taking little pause breaks throughout her busy day. Then she needed to practise the following techniques for dealing with anger.

Anger Releasing Techniques

Examine your hot buttons; those trigger points that activate you. Look at the things others do that bother you. List them one at a time on a piece of paper. Ask yourself, *"Do I do this?"* with each one. Write out your answer. Then, ask yourself the following questions:

What do I need to see about me?
Is there an opportunity for healing here?
When I was little, did anyone do this to me? If so who and when?
What can I learn from this situation, this person?
How can I use this information to grow?

Give yourself plenty of response time. Sit with your awareness and wonders will occur. You will get to know yourself on a more intimate level and you will become part of the solution instead of deepening the problem.[1]

---

1 Should you want to go further, and learn how to deal with flare-ups, hot flashes, dropping the anger ball, stopping the blame-game and learning how to express anger in a healthy manner, get a copy of my book: *Celebrating Anger—Creative Solutions for Managing Conflict at Home, on the Job, and in Relationships.*

Celebration Strategies

1. Dealing with other people's anger

If you have trouble dealing with someone else's anger, particularly with rising voices, criticism or yelling, here's a tip: think of their anger as thunder. Just let it roll. Don't get caught up in the storm! Avoid taking it personally. Wait until they've vented, then, if you need to, declare your boundary, using I language. For example, "I appreciate that you are feeling frustrated, however please keep your voice down when you speak to me."

If someone tries to harm you *physically*, head for the hills! Get out of the situation as quickly as possible. There are shelters and programs available to help you do this.

2. Handling difficult people

As for handling difficult people, statistics tell us one out of three is a difficult person, so try this. The next time you're in a lineup at the grocery store, or you find yourself with any group of people, look to your right, look to your left, look down at your navel then determine who you think might be that one in three.

We're all difficult people, depending on who's doing the describing. If you live or work with a difficult personality, here are strategies for dealing with him/her.

a. Acknowledge them.

Make sure your voice is calm and, if possible, friendly, for example, *"I can see you're really upset about this."* Breathe, and wait for their response. Keep breathing.

b. Give them time to vent

Let them express their frustration, and make sure you just listen. Don't interrupt or try to defend. Listen.

c. Empathize.

"I imagine you feel _____." [fill in the blank]. Don't tell them what they're feeling, or they'll snap at you again. None of us like to be told what we're feeling.

d. Ask.

Ask them what they'd like to do—how they want to deal with the situation—and wait for their response.

e. Affirm.

Affirm their best choice. And, give yourself a pat on the back as well.

That's all there is to it. You've been able to help someone deal with his/her anger, and you haven't been caught by it yourself . . . or have you? Well, remember, no matter how much work we do on ourselves, we're still human. So, give your self an A for effort and bring out the welcome mat for anger.

3. A timely tip

It might not be the best time to confront someone when you feel agitated. Take time to look at what is going on with you, breathe, and wait until you feel peaceful. Then you'll be in a much better position to deal with someone else.

Anger is only an emotion, one you need not be afraid of. When you acknowledge that you have that tiger inside, you can tame it by identifying your triggers, using anger-releasing techniques and putting your celebration strategies to work. When you respect anger and use it as a catalyst for your own growth, it will serve you well.

Affirmation: Today, I am willing to deal with anger.
Today, I am ready for growth!

Six

Acceptance

I exist as I am, and that is enough. If no other in the world be aware, I sit content, and if each and all be aware, I sit content.
Walt Whitman

The harder we try to catch hold of the moment, to seize a pleasant sensation . . . the more elusive it becomes. It is like trying to clutch water in one's hands—the harder one grips, the faster it slips through one's fingers.
Alan Watts

Life is what happens while you're busy making other plans.
John Lennon

When I was a teenager hiding out in the movies, I yearned to be brilliant and sophisticated like Katherine Hepburn. I wanted to be the girl next door like Sally Fields. I wanted to be sultry and sexy like Liz Taylor. More than anything, I wanted to be *not me*, living my *not life*. So, I watched movies and fantasized.

I spent many years disowning myself. By 16, I was tall, blonde, slim-hipped and full breasted—but all I could think of was that my hair curled, and I wanted it straight. Every day I'd iron my hair straight, then get frustrated when it started to wave three hours later. My youngest daughter went through the same thing in her adolescence—twisting herself into a pretzel as she tried to be what the fashion magazines dictated, slapping on make-up, straightening her hair, trying to be anyone but herself.

Adolescence can be painful, for it's a time when many of us crave acceptance by our pears, and some of us continue this craving long past adolescence.

Believing I was somehow defective, I searched through novels, films and magazines, seeking clues on how to look. I dressed like this one, stood like another. Copied entrances and exits, smoked because it seemed sophisticated and pretended I was a movie queen.

I lived in fantasy.

In clubs I ordered martinis or scotch on the rocks and perched on a bar stool, surveying the scene through a foggy haze, tossing my tawny mane around like I'd seen in the movies.

At 21, I met and married a man who complemented my image. He was tall, dark and handsome—perfect! He was also intense, intelligent, well read and foreign. How exotic! Most importantly, he wanted me. He appeared and sounded impressive and I felt validated. Not once did I consider whether it was a good match, whether we were complementary in character or whether we shared similar values. All that counted was the rush of excitement I felt when I was with him, which I interpreted as love.

I doubt if I had any thoughts about what he needed either and at the time I believed I was a deep thinker. Actually,

I was scared and confused.

I had no role models of married people and I didn't have the foggiest notion of who I was. I knew I had to fit into the marriage box somehow, and he seemed a fine candidate. Because he wanted me, I thought it meant I was valuable. Somehow I would know what to do as a married lady, and we'd live happily. I put on the white dress and said, "I do" believing that I'd be safe and secure. The handsome prince had rescued Cinderella.

Looking back, I see how naïve I was. My husband and I were both strong-willed people with a "my way or the highway" attitude. For the first few years, I deferred to his wishes, having babies, staying at home and learning how to cook and clean. After five years, I was going stir-crazy. I had ideas of my own and wanted more freedom and a career.

Our wills collided and the marriage started to erode. I had no training in diplomacy; no idea of how to make a marriage work. What I knew was how to fight, point the blame finger and run away. Inevitably, the marriage fell apart and I began the search for a new partner. I wasn't ready to self-examine or to ask myself what I needed and what I had to offer. I was in too much of a hurry in those days, thinking that if the right man would just materialize and kiss me quick, like sleeping beauty I'd awaken and live happily ever after.

It took years before I was able to stop running and pretending—to slow down long enough so I could begin looking at me. And then I had to do it on the heels of defeat.

Have you noticed we seem to learn more in the valleys of life than on the mountaintops? And what we think of as the worst times often turn out to be our biggest turning points?

I was in a particularly low valley when I began to embrace the notion that

I'd made a mess of my life.

I didn't have a clue about who I was or what I was doing, let alone any idea of how to live. I had to accept that I'd harmed myself, neglected my children and verbally abused my partners. I had to live with that awareness. I wasn't the golden girl. I wasn't a princess in disguise or a movie queen. I was a person who lived in fantasy and pretended to be someone she was not. I was someone who dreamed, then drank her dreams away. I'd blown precious years with my children because I'd been obsessed with finding love instead of giving it. I'd run from responsibilities because I thought everything important was "out there." I had to face myself and I didn't enjoy doing it.

And yet, when I was able to see myself as I truly was, I felt some relief, as if I'd been able to lay some of my burdens down. It was good to acknowledge that I wasn't a saint in hiding or a discovery about to happen. I was just another person with both good and not-so-good traits. I started shedding the fantasy image and gave up trying to be perfect, or living according to some ideal. I became real-sized instead of aiming for larger-than-life.

Today, I'm authentically me, for better or worse. I'm the only one I'll have a lifelong relationship with, so it makes sense to let the real me hang out. The only time I revert to old behavior is when I get nervous, because I'm in a new or uncomfortable situation. Automatically, I step into the role of entertainer or interviewer as a coping mechanism. But even that impulse is fading.

Now I weigh 10 more pounds than I once did and have lines on my face. I accept who I am: just another person on this planet, doing the best I can with what I've got. This acceptance gives me the freedom to accept others as they are, because I know that we are all just human. You may be a different color, sex or shape than I, but you are just you. You may be differently abled than I am, and have different challenges and issues to deal with, but the thing is, when I can accept me as I am, then I can accept you. And if you can accept you as you are, then you can accept me. And if we both do this, we have a good shot at creating an honest relationship.

Living Life on Life's Terms

One of the great secrets of happiness is being able to accept one another *exactly* the way we are and live life on life's terms, like my friend Kerry does.

Kerry is a 68-year-old artist. Divorced at an early age, Kerry raised her only son Charlie the best way she knew how. "I wasn't perfect by any means, but I know I've done everything I could to make him strong. I fed him well and gave him vitamins to make his body strong. I was a loving, caring mother. I gave him as much as I could." Now 38, Charlie has been diagnosed with Huntington's disease, a neurological disorder for which there is no cure. Huntington's kills brain cells indiscriminately, so that every organ in the body is affected. "You can live with Huntington's for a long time. Normally, it's fatal at about 11 years." Huntington's first affected Charlie when he was about 29.

Kerry informed me that Huntington's is hereditary and each generation becomes affected younger than the generation before. In other words, Charlie's children are at risk and might see signs of it in their early 20s. Here's how Kerry describes living with the knowledge that her only son has Huntington's.

I live a day at a time—sometimes, an hour at a time. One of the biggest things I do to keep my sanity is to realize that Charlie's not dead, and I don't want to bury him before he's ready to lie down. He celebrates life! He drove his jeep all over the country, and now he's got a sailboat. He told me that he wanted to show his kids how to live with Huntington's. He said he thought his dad took the coward's way out. [Charlie's father, who suffered from Huntington's, committed suicide when he was 47, and Charlie was 20.]

Charlie started exhibiting symptoms six years ago. He was holding his hands, putting his arm on top of a chair so it wouldn't shake. Eventually, we talked about it. He is determined that it won't rule his life. He won't give into it in any area. Charlie tries to live as normal a life as he can. He sees his two kids from a former marriage on a regular basis.

I have to tell you that Huntington's has colored my life for the last 35 years, both with Charlie and his dad. There's no getting around it. It's a cruel illness. It robs people of their personhood. Long before Charlie dies, he will be dead as a person. I can handle the jerking around of the body, but seeing his personality change; that's hard. For example, right now, Charlie's sensitivity and kindness are getting overruled by his anger at having this disease. I know this will pass, but then something else will come up.

What I think is most important is to deal with this or any other disease one day at a time, and to really practise gratitude for what is today. If I start to think of it all as a loss, then I'm lost! Charlie doesn't feel that way, so what right do I have to? I can't be moaning and groaning about my son. I really have to look at him as an adult man and give him adult respect. I'm content that he's handling it as well as anyone could. Losing someone on the installment plan does not make it easier. My dad died over a three-year period, and it was still a blow.

I have to work at living in the day, accepting that this is the way it is. If I project, I'm in dire straits. I have to live my life. It's up to me to make it whatever I want it to be. If I do my part, like accept the situation the way it is, and leave the rest alone, we'll all be better off!

The Challenge of Acceptance

Accepting the illness, the mortality of our own children, has got to be one of the hardest things a parent can do. And the bravest. Kerry moved out West to look after Charlie. Whenever I talk with her on the telephone I'm amazed at her sense of humor and her acceptance of this increasingly difficult situation. Even when our children are healthy, acceptance can be challenging.

Anna is a single parent. Her only child, Blaine, is now 14. Raising a son alone is no picnic, but Blaine has always been a good kid—until now. Now, he's different: sulky, moody, unresponsive, private.

Anna is driving herself crazy, wanting to check his bureau drawers for dope, spy over his shoulder when he's on the Internet, and inspect under his mattress to see if he's hiding porn magazines or condoms. At the same time, she doesn't want to invade his privacy. She knows that she needs to accept Blaine as he is, a hormonal teenager. She wants to maintain their good communication, and take charge of her emotions. She's just beginning menopause and finds herself victim to sudden angry outbursts and fear-driven fantasies, as she worries and obsesses about Blaine.

Do you think it's some kind of cosmic joke that many women enter menopause just when their children reach adolescence—when hormones are raging in both? Perhaps it is an opportunity for each generation to discover what's similar, instead of taking opposing positions.

Price versus Payoff

In any relationship, there's a price and a payoff. We need to accept that the price we pay is for the payoff we want—beforehand, if possible. Laura, for example, likes younger men. She finds them more open and sexy; that is her payoff. She doesn't like feeling older, however, so she gets caught in a trap of wanting the younger man to have the same amount of experience that she does and when he doesn't, she gets frustrated and disillusioned, that is her price.

I know people who complain about the price but they still want the payoff. I think we need to be clear upfront about what is acceptable and what is not. We need to lay our cards face up on the table so we know what we've got to work with. We need to make a list of pros and cons and see how long each list is. Then we can

decide what we can live with, and what we cannot.

Personally, I would rather be in relationship than not be, which means I have to make adjustments and work on acceptance. When I'm critical of *him,* I need to look at what's going on with *me.*

Acceptance is not easy. It was a lot easier living on my own, but there wasn't as much growth or fun. The price I pay for being in a relationship is small compared to the payoffs I receive. In the process, I've expanded my ability to be patient and loving. I believe each of us needs to determine what we want, or will accept from another person, then live with that. This means knowing our own needs, wants and habits.

The other day, Sue called to tell me how upset she was because Betty, a mutual friend was, in Sue's words, "invalidating her experience." Can anyone invalidate our experience? I don't think so, yet sometimes it feels like they can. What Sue later realized was that there was a part of herself that was invalidating her *own* experience. When Betty verbally undermined her, Sue felt diminished. She needed to tell Betty that what was so for her was so. Then, no one could invalidate her feelings.

Why do so many of us tell each other what to do and how to do it, especially when we start living together? Perhaps it comes from repeating parental patterns or vying for power. We interpret what such-and-such means, or what life should be like for someone else. We speak as if we had inside information and a pipeline to God. Women in particular fall into this trap. We put enormous energy into men—fashioning them, coaching them—and then wonder why we feel depleted, or why they are resistant to us and want to escape. Is it because we've given our energy and our power away? Might it be more rewarding if we spent that energy doing what we need to do to make our own lives fulfilling?

In my counselling practice, I've seen many women do the emotional work for their men and feel resentful about it. One woman was angry because, as she put it, *"he gets away with everything, and flies high and free like a bird"* while she carried his emotional baggage and felt heavy. That reminds me of the story of the woman who was drowning and watched her *husband's* life flash before her eyes!

Years ago, I saw a play called, *For Colored Girls Only Who Sing The Blues.* In one scene, a woman stomps around the stage crying, *"He stole my stuff, he stole my stuff, and now I have nothing!"* This scene stayed with me because, at the time, I was living with a very beautiful young man whom I'd been grooming for perfection. I'd taught him how to dress, what books to read, which music to listen to, and the correct wines to order. I'd spent countless hours devoting myself to his education, and for what? So I could have the perfect man for me, of course! The thing was, I felt exhausted from the effort, and bored with the result. Then, guess what happened? He became assured and confident and one day he walked out of my house and into the arms of someone else. And there I was, empty, angry and worn out.

I could hardly blame him for what I'd created! The conclusion I later came to was that he'd been fine just as he was, before I started re-arranging him. I can see that now, but then I was trying to live up to the socially correct appearance of what I imagined others would accept, instead of being grateful for how he was. This was a harsh lesson.

In my imaginings, I think I want a mate who is there for my every whim, who understands me perfectly, who deeply loves me yet does not impose on me very much—rather like a pet. But, would I really want a relationship like that? Would you?

Gradually I've come to understand that trying to change other people is futile, foolish and certainly not loving.

It doesn't trust that they have their own path to walk, and their own lessons to learn, difficult and painful as some of those lessons might be. Now I think that love means letting those we love be themselves, and not trying to make them fit our picture.

Do I walk my talk? Sometimes yes, and sometimes no. I work at living my own life and try to let others do the same. I am in the habit of being bossy, so I have to catch myself when I get on a roll and mentally tape my mouth shut. I have a habit, you see, and it's called control.

Habits are hard to break: possible, but difficult. For example, I used to smoke cigarettes. For many years, I enjoyed my cigarette habit, then I tried quitting and couldn't. I was addicted. When my bronchial tubes began complaining and I developed a nasty smoker's cough, I decided that the price was too high, and I quit. The way I did this was by substitution. Instead of smoking as I sipped my morning coffee, I began reading inspirational books. Instead of sitting down with a cigarette, I went for walks after dinner. I replaced life-depleting rituals with life-generating ones and gradually these became enjoyable new habits.

Lately I've started eating at night when I watch television and the pounds are beginning to add up. Once again, I'm applying the price/payoff formula. I do not want to gain any more weight, so I've come up with four options. I can:

- massage my feet while I watch television,
- leave the room during food commercials (but stay out of the kitchen.)
- read
- take an evening exercise class.

To inspire me I've put a slogan on my refrigerator that reads "Nothing tastes as good as being thin feels."

We all have undesirable habits. As a society, we're addicted to escapism through eating, watching television, drinking, taking drugs, shopping, ingesting caffeine, working, etc. The list is endless. The only successful way I've ever found to break an unwanted habit is to substitute a better one. But first we have to accept that we have this unattractive habit. We must look it straight in the eye, and ask what we're avoiding *seeing* or *doing*.

Victim or Victor? It's Your Choice

Everybody has some challenge, some situation that affects him or her. We need to make a decision. Do we want to be a victim of this habit or a victor? If we want to be victorious, then we can make an action plan.

We can take charge and make changes.

We can trade our comfortable habit in for something that will enliven us and make us feel good about ourselves.

Recently, I caught myself giving my husband "the look" because we were dining out and he was eating with his elbows on the table. A small detail, yet one that annoyed me. I felt myself tightening up, wanting to take his arm down, falling into the "mother" role. I know I can't change him, but in that moment I sure wanted to make some adjustments. It was price and payoff time again. Excusing myself, I went to the washroom and had a little chat with me. Why was it important that he eat a certain way? I looked at my motive, my need to do things in what I considered a proper way. Proper for whom, I asked myself. Did I respect his right to eat the way he chooses? Did I really want him to be a clone of me? How big a deal was this? Could I accept it as one of the things he does that I wish he didn't, but can live with, like the way he accepts me biting my nails when we watch a movie? Yes, I could. I returned to the table and enjoyed the rest of the meal.

You may think this is terribly petty, but I've learned

it's the small things that build up and later cause us grief.

Those little annoyances, which, like mosquito bites, become itchy, so we scratch them or pick at them until they fester and become bigger. When I physically or mentally walk away from the situation and have an internal conversation with myself, it's a way of taking the stinger out and reminding myself that acceptance is the name of my game. Then I can think of all the wonderful things my fellow does, like facilitating creative workshops, making beautiful shelves, giving me massages that are to die for, and being nonjudgmental and encouraging.

When I focus on the positive payoffs, it creates freedom for us both. I concentrate on doing what I need to do and let him be. I pay attention to my own needs instead of fixing someone else up, hoping they'll appreciate my efforts.

I like the prose poem Fritz Perls wrote that was popular in the 1970s:

I do my thing, and you do your thing. I am not in this world to live up to your expectations, and you are not in this world to live up to mine. You are you and I am I, and if by chance we find each other, it's beautiful. Even if we don't find each other, it's beautiful if we find ourselves.

Expectations of others have consistently been my downfall. Whenever I expect anyone to act or be a certain way, I set myself up for heartache.

Toby, my Siamese cat, teaches me acceptance. When we're at the cottage, Toby brings me trophies and gifts in the form of half-dead chipmunks, birds or mice. I shriek and yell at him, trying to save what's left of the animal, trying to dissuade him from killing, wanting Toby to be only the sweet loving cat who curls up beside me at night, and not the vicious predator he becomes outdoors. Toby sits there, conquest in his mouth, looking at me as if I'm demented, which I am, of course! I have to accept that he is a cat and a hunter, as well as an affectionate pet. He shows different aspects of his being, just like people do.

Acceptance brings freedom. This applies to accepting the weather, the traffic, the state of the nation and our own limitations. Accepting a situation doesn't mean being passive about it. We can still choose to do something about it. Change our attitude, if that's what's needed, or pick up the telephone. We can join a committee and be part of the solution.

What about you? Would you like some help with acceptance? Try out the Three A's below.

Angela's Excellent Acceptance Techniques

The Three A's are essential techniques for developing acceptance. The three A's are easy to remember. They come at the beginning of the alphabet. You can use one A at a time, or apply them in sequence. Every time you use them you're making progress. Besides, most of us want to get an A in something, in *or* out of school. Here's how you can use the three A's.

The Three A's

1. Awareness

The first A stands for *awareness*. Become aware of how you think and feel. Notice your thoughts. Identify patterns. Notice feelings, locating them in your body. Notice your reactions, as if you were a witness to yourself, just noticing.

2. Acknowledge

Once you become aware of your thoughts and behavior patterns, you're ready to acknowledge this is how you really are. For some, this is a stretch, because it shatters our illusions of perfection. That's a good thing. We can't really change ourselves in any significant way until we know ourselves, so this becomes your challenge: to fully acknowledge who you are and how you express yourself.

3. Action

The third A stands for *action*. Take whatever action you need to practise acceptance. It could be simply breathing awareness in and out of your body. It could be reminding yourself that your thoughts create matter. As neurobiologist Dr. Candice Pert has proven, neuropeptides (the chemicals triggered by emotions) are thoughts converted into matter, which means our emotions get stored in our bodies and often become diseases which later plague us. Remembering the mind/body connection can help us dispel the initial thought. We can say *"cancel, cancel"* to our fear thought, our negative reaction, and substitute a positive. thought or an acceptance blessing. We do this because we want to take care of ourselves.

Whether the acceptance blessing is for us or for someone else is immaterial. The situation is offering us an opportunity to give love, to create healing. Taking action to transform our thoughts enables us to retain our power instead of squandering it. Blessing others opens the door to our own integration. When we send another thoughts of compassion or peace-of-mind, we receive the same! Then, we can take some playful action, for example, saying or singing, *"I accept me and I accept you do-de-le-do-de-le-do,"* over and over again. We could write an acceptance letter to ourselves and read it aloud every day. We could look in the mirror, gaze into our own eyes and tell ourselves *"I accept you just the way you are."*

One positive action leads to another, and then another. After all the struggling of non-acceptance, all those attempts at trying to be perfect, to please, to fit in, being able to accept ourselves is a great relief. And it takes time, so give yourself time and plenty of encouragement. Think of it like learning how to walk. We do it by putting one foot in front of another and taking one baby step at a time.

When we are able to accept ourselves, as is, then we are equipped to accept others as they are. Acceptance of humanity, of both the good and shadow sides we each have, keeps us humble. Through acceptance comes a deeper understanding of how we each get caught in our own web of expectations, and this under-standing can breed compassion. With compassion, we can begin to extend our understanding to one another and use it to heal our individual families and our troubled world.

Acceptance is a skill everyone can learn. I would like to see it taught in every school and practiced routinely on a daily basis.

Human beings, by changing the inner attitudes of their minds, can change the outer aspects of their lives.
William James

I had to accept my own character defects—and I have many of them—then roll up my sleeves and get to work on *me*. I had to let go of expecting my mother to change. I had to give up the notion of the fantasy mom I wanted, the one who would say she loved me and be affectionate. I had to accept my mother as she was, and love her as best as I could. I had to let go of wanting my brother to move back to Canada, and accept him where he is, living in England, doing what he is doing. I had to accept my children and grandchildren as they are, and love them on their journey, and not as if they were supposed to have completed it.

This meant I couldn't give advice unless I was asked. It also meant I could ask for what I needed, such as no smoking in the cottage when they came to visit, and respecting my quiet time in the morning.

Acceptance Takes Practice!

Through practising acceptance, I have witnessed many changes in my own life. I have accepted that I will never be a finished product, and instead am truly a work in progress. I'm free to be fully myself, free to make decisions that enrich my life, free to let other people live the lives they are meant to live. And, when I blow it, I am free to acknowledge my errors and just get on with learning. As the Liberian proverb instructs "Do not look where you fell, but where you slipped."

Celebration Strategies

How to practise acceptance

1. Appraise

Make an in-depth inventory of yourself. List your character assets and debits. If you're not sure what these are, ask your friends or colleagues what they like or admire about you and what they don't like, too. Ask your kids. Listen to what they have to say. Once you have a list, go to the mirror, look into your own eyes and read your list. When you are finished, speak to your mirror image. Say something like:

"This is me, and I accept me as I am. I know that only through self-acceptance do I grow and flourish, never by self-rejection."

Make sure you stand there for at least a full minute after you say this, so you can take the truth in.

You could speak to your mirror image every day for a month to strengthen your self-love. You could also share your list with a trusted friend or counsellor. When we're able to share what we don't like about ourselves with another, we become more self-accepting.

2. Assess

Think about the person(s) you don't accept. Whom do you criticize and judge? Write out the person's name and the specific actions you object to.

3. Ask

Ask yourself: *"Do I do this?"* Try to be totally truthful.

4. Accept

Practise working the acceptance strategies on yourself and others. Use the 3 A's: Awareness, Acknowledge and Action. Try doing this just for today. This is your time on earth; there may not be another time, so why waste another second in non-acceptance?

5. Affirm

Repeatedly say, *"I am free to be me."* Say it softly to yourself and say it aloud. Write or speak the affirmation below.

The act of acceptance can be difficult but revealing. Learning to accept yourself as well as others is a worthwhile exercise; it can give you more flexibility and an openness to new people, experiences and opportunities. By silencing that negative inner voice, you just might be able to grab hold of what you've been missing. Give yourself a pat on the back every time you catch yourself accepting you or others just a teeny bit more. Celebrate your successes!

Affirmation: Today I love and accept myself exactly as I am.

Seven

Find Forgiveness

Everyone thinks of changing the world,
but no one thinks of changing himself.
Leo Tolstoy

Nothing we do, however virtuous,
can be accomplished alone.
Therefore, we are saved by love.
Reinhold Niebuhr

Forgiveness. Forgiveness.
Even if you don't love me anymore.
Don Henley

I'll never forgive him, never. There I was, having our baby in the
hospital, and he was nowhere to be found. Later, I discovered he'd
been with some girl he'd picked up in a bar. I mean . . . go figure!
Well, the baby and I are doing just fine, thank you, and he's calling
every day, begging me to forgive him, to take him back but I won't.
Joanne, 23

She moved out West with me and, while I had money, everything was great. We were on cloud nine. We found a great apartment, and she furnished it beautifully. Then my money ran out and the next day, I mean the very next day, she was gone. That was it. All the wedding plans went down the drain. She took the diamond engagement ring I'd given her. Took the artwork and all the clothes of course. She left me a note saying: "Sorry. Hope things get better for you, love . . ." Love? Who's kidding whom! Anyway, I hear she's not doing so well, and you know what? I'm glad. I know that sounds ugly, but the truth is, I hope she falls flat on her face. Forgive her? No way!

Adam, 35

I left home at 14. My mother had taken to smashing me in the face with her fist by then, and I was afraid that the next time she did it, I'd kill her. One night I snuck out of the house and hit the road. I made my way to the city and I've done all right since then. I went back for my father's funeral 10 years ago, and left as soon as the service was over. For all I know she's dead now too.

Pete, 46

I don't know if I can forgive him. He's old now, and pathetic. I've hated him most of my life, for what he did to me and my sister. Now I'm getting older myself, and it seems like a lot of effort to hate him. Besides, he's all the family I have left. I just don't know anymore.

Dolores, 53

Forgiveness is tough. It does not come easily to many of us. There's a payoff in nursing grudges, pointing out injustices and attributing our lack of success to parents, spouses, our environment and circumstance. We get to keep the old habit of pointing accusatory fingers at others and at the same time we stay secure in our comfort zone of feeling justified for doing so. But, just like when our computers go wonky when we overload them, *our* internal drive—our hearts and our minds—can become saturated with grievances and every so often, we need to clear out the clutter.

I have struggled with forgiveness. I had to get to the point where I realized that each grievance I held took a little more energy from me; every resentment I nurtured kept me imprisoned. When this truth finally hit home, I decided to do something about it once and for all. I made a list of my grudges—every one of them—writing out the names and events of all the people I thought had hurt or maligned me. This took quite a while. When I felt complete with my list, I began to look at what my part was in the situation. What had I done? Where had I contributed? What had I said? I asked myself these questions because I knew it was for my own benefit. I longed to become whole and integrated, instead of staying splintered by holding onto grievances. I wanted more interior space.

Have you ever noticed that when you start to work on one of your personal shortcomings, the universe responds by giving you more of whatever it is you're trying to work on?

One summer I rented a small oceanfront cottage and invited my eldest daughter and both grandkids to visit me for a week. I pictured us doing beach and kid things in the daytime, then having chatty evenings playing games together and becoming closer. I love my daughter dearly and long for more intimacy with her. I reckoned this holiday would be my opportunity to create a special family experience.

Can you detect an expectation here?

My daughter had a different agenda. She readily admits that she has kept herself distant from me. That's the history. On this occasion she wanted to read, which would have been fine if I could have hung out with the kids. But she wanted to read and keep the kids beside her, while maintaining a physical distance from me. I sat further along the beach, watching the three of them reading, feeling excruciating sadness. I could sense my anger mounting, so I walked over to where my daughter was sitting and attempted to tell her what was going on for me.

"Look Mom, I'm not interested in that touchy feely stuff," she replied. Then, glancing into my teary eyes, she said: "You know, Mom, I may never be the daughter you want," and returned to her book.

I walked away and realized, with chagrin, that I was probably not the mother she wanted either. That possibility got me thinking.

I thought about my own mother, who had also maintained her distance. I got a mental picture of me standing in the park when I was seven years old, watching my mother push my little brother on the swing; me on the sidelines, watching and yearning for love. Wanting to be pushed but being told I was "too old." Sitting in the park and suffering with unfulfilled longing.

I had harbored anger and fermented resentments towards my mother for many years, secretly blaming her for splitting up with my dad. I'd held her responsible for my loss of family and subsequent years of abusive foster homes. All of this landed at my mother's feet because, somehow, she was *supposed* to have prevented this or at least handled it better. It was part of her job as a mother!

It had never occurred to me that perhaps I'd had a larger need for love than she could fill.

Great Expectations

Have you ever had a script for someone who simply wouldn't play the role? Did you hang onto hurts long past the doing? Have you promised yourself you'd never love that deeply again, that you were better off without the person? Have you walled up your heart?

Holding my mother for emotional ransom was much more about me than it was about her. Once I realized this, I was able to make some headway in forgiving her while she was still alive.

Heck, she was old and it didn't make any sense to keep on punishing her by dredging up the past.

Now my daughter has me as a mother, with my history of being erratic. Inconsistent at paying attention to her needs, I'd alternated between showering affection upon her, then being oblivious to her presence. She must have felt confused and angry, and now it was payback time. *"What did I expect from her?"* I asked myself. It was time for an adjustment—mine!

I had to release the antagonism I was feeling towards my daughter, so, I headed back to the cottatge, called a friend and cried on the telephone. She suggested that maybe I didn't need to set myself up with my daughter again, and I really heard her. I spent some time pondering what that would look like. Then I began to concentrate on the wonderful qualities my daughter exhibits and wrote out an appreciation list. What got put on that list? Her liveliness, her generosity and her ability to get going and just do whatever needed doing. Her style and oomph, her fabulous talent with clothing, her flair, her smarts, her savvy and her shrewdness too.

I think she is amazing. I get a kick out of being with her and I love her. That's the truth. I love her.

I've heard that real love is unconditional. My daughter is not supposed to be the same as me. It is quite enough that she is she. So I began releasing my picture of how our holiday should be, and started accepting her as she was, and that opened up my heart.

I could feel a space within me expanding, as the constriction I'd held around both my mother and my daughter began to ease. It was *my* constriction after all, and my choice to let it go—to forgive them both for real or imagined hurts.

My daughter is my teacher. Have you noticed that our kids, our partners and our grandchildren are our very best teachers?

What I have learned about forgiveness is that it really is FOR me to GIVE. It is both my agony and my bliss.

When I am consumed with negativity over another's behavior, I have lost my focus. I don't have to accept behavior that is intolerable, but wallowing in negativity does not alter the situation. Instead of using forgiveness as an eraser to wipe another's page clean, I think of forgiveness as scissors that I use to cut the strings of resentment that bind me to a grievance or to a hurt.

Keeping resentments towards another is like taking poison and hoping the other person will die!

Every time I try to tighten the noose of resentment around someone else's neck, I am really choking myself. When I snip the resentment with my forgiveness scissors, I set myself free.

I'm a hothead and get defensive quickly. So, when I'm triggered, I need to apply my anger tools. Then I can read serenity reminders found in my daily meditation books, ask for help and talk about my struggles with others. That's the way I get through them. It doesn't work for me to ignore the situation or to pretend it doesn't matter. That just becomes rotting compost for resentments to grow inside of me—resentment tumors I call them—and they're lethal.

It doesn't help me to plot revenge or keep a score card of wrong doings; when I do this I compound the problem and hurt myself and anyone else in my path. Confronting my daughter only creates more distance between us. I'm learning to do what I can to look after me, and accept her as is.

I hope the day will come when we can talk freely but, if it doesn't, I can live with it. I can appreciate her even from a distance. I can be grateful she is in my life, which does not mean that I don't need to set boundaries. As George Herbert advises, "Love your neighbor, yet pull not down your hedge."

All I know is, today, I love her and feel at peace within myself. That's what forgiveness gives to me. It renders me whole.

Our Histories Shape Us

Forgiving means to be for giving, not for hating or retaliating. To accomplish this, we need to remove whatever darkness we've let into our psyche, and allow the light of love fill up that space. Then we need to think of something positive about that person, and concentrate on it. This is not easy to do, but it is possible.

I really believe that we need to forgive the things that happened to us in the first half of our lives—the people we believed failed us, and the ways we failed ourselves—in order to live fully in the second half of our lives.

We all have a history.

We have sad stories to tell and people to forgive. The only question is; when will we do it? For me, this has meant reflecting upon my life and looking at the ways I've held back my love, thinking I was "showing them."

It began with my mother. Once I accepted that she wasn't the mother I wanted her to be, I could look at who she was. I didn't have a mother who kept her family together like some women do after their husbands leave. I had a mother who did the best she could with what she had. I needed to understand life from her perspective, even though she couldn't help me do this.

Searching out her past, finding the few voices that remembered her, I imagined what it must have been like for her, dealing with the losses she'd had. When she was barely 13, my mother came home from school one afternoon to find her own mother's charred body being wheeled out of the house. Lillian, my grandmother, had rescued a neighboring child who had somehow dropped her rag doll too close to the fireplace. The doll caught fire, the child's dress was ignited, and my grandmother, who bravely saved this little girl, paid with her own life.

After her mother's death, my mother Audrey and her younger brother Earle were sent to a different city to live with a maiden aunt who did not like children.

Three years later, they moved back with their father but that summer he slipped off the roof he was repairing, fell three stories and broke his neck. My mother had just turned 16 when she became an orphan. Three years later, Earle drowned in a logging accident. By the time she was 20, her entire family was wiped out. I cannot pretend to know what those tragedies did to her mind and spirit.

She met and married my charming dad when she was 21. At first, they lived an exciting life, throwing lavish parties, traveling extensively, and being written up in the local gossip columns. During those early years, my mother repeatedly tried to have children but each time she got pregnant she miscarried. I was born when she was 31.

Always a private person, my mother kept herself tightly bound, refusing to discuss her family and her losses. Today I understand how traumatized she must have been. She probably was afraid to talk about her history, afraid that if the floodgates opened, there would be no end to her grief. Keeping her own counsel, being spartan with words, my mother probably didn't praise my father very often, and he was a man who needed admiration.

There must have been a part of her that expected to be let down, a secret suspicion that she was jinxed. So it happened. My father ran off with a younger woman, leaving my mother with children, debts and no money. Having no family of her own, my mother turned to my father's married but childless brother and his spinster sister. They said they'd each take one of us on the condition that they could adopt us. My mother would not hear of it. Undoubtedly at her wits' end but too proud to go on welfare, she got a job and found foster homes for Nick and me.

It must have seemed to her that there was no end to suffering. I imagine it took all her strength to dissolve the household and go to work. I'm sure she thought she'd be able to get us back sooner than she did. Perhaps she simply didn't have anything left to give anyone, so she paid the foster fee and visited us every two weeks. She did that for six years, then I went to live with her. I can tell you, I must have been hell on wheels.

When I look at my mother from this perspective, I have a sense of how devastated she must have been, how wounded. When I think about her life, my own dark veil of pain lifts, and I can make room for poignant memories of her walking down the street when she came to visit. I can see her sweet blue eyes and remember how she patiently listened, head cocked, silently attentive. I can feel the love I have kept encased and, for so many years, denied. I remember her moving into a larger apartment so she could bring us to live with her. Many nights I would see her sewing late into the night, making party dresses for me. I can picture her at the job she kept for 27 years, until she had a stroke, which left her partially paralyzed at 63.

I caught a special glimpse of her after that stroke when she sat in a hospital bed. My brother Nick sat on the chair beside her—the two of them simply sitting and sharing a comfortable silence together, their alikeness transparent.

I remember her smoking and holding forth in her recliner chair, choosing her words carefully, gesticulating with her slim, long, manicured fingers. Her acerbic tongue and clever wit punctuated her sentences, and her melodious voice was fluid, like the piano music she once played.

There are gifts she gave me, like the adage, *"if at first you don't succeed, try, try again."* I have forged my life from this perspective.

I remember the quiet gentleness and infinite patience my mother exhibited; the way she held her tongue. She never bad-mouthed or gossiped about anyone. She'd just grit her teeth and say, *"Silence is golden."* And I, her daughter, became a public speaker, talking whenever I could. It must have been difficult for her to have a daughter like me.

I was her mouthpiece. I told the secrets.

I have learned much from my mother's example, and have a great deal to emulate and be grateful for in her legacy of character. I have much to forgive myself for as well; I harbored grudges towards her when she was alive and, although I made some gains on this with her, I was not reconciled the way I am now.

Time is a great healer.

I chose to forgive my father. To understand that he was so caught up in his own personal mythology that he couldn't see the hurt he inflicted on others. My father, William George, was the sixth and last child of a strict and religious family. He was given the name of the firstborn son who died as an infant. My father was supposed to make up for that loss. He was supposed to be the best and the most: the family savior.

I know he tried. I remember his powerful presence, and the way others would grin when they thought about him. They told me he lit up every room he entered. His humor and high spirits were legendary. My father's affection sustained me long after he was gone. The fact that he'd held me and told me he loved me mattered. I knew what love was, or at least what affection was. I could feel it, and wanted more. This longing enabled me to both search for and express that same affection to others.

My father was bold and elegant. Sporting monogrammed white shirts under navy pinstriped suits, he flashed a silver cigarette case, kept crisp one hundred dollar bills in his wallet, and always drove a white Jaguar. He told exuberant stories and sang inspirational songs. He encouraged me to recite poetry, to sing and to perform for his friends. These early demonstrations sowed seeds and motivated me to share my own inspirational stories with friends and, later, audiences. I would not be able to do the work I do without my father's example.

He could only go so far in his own life. He became ensnared in alcoholism—that web of deception and denial. I can understand this because I suffered from the same affliction and well remember thinking my fantasies were real. He was a good marker for me for I knew what would happen if I followed in his footsteps.

Today I can accept the legacy my father left me, and use these gifts in a spirit of celebration. I am indeed my father's daughter, and in my own personality I try to marry his fiery attributes with the more genteel qualities of my mother.

Forgiveness means forgiving *and* forgetting.

I've had to forgive the foster father who sexually abused me. First, I needed to let out the rage I felt at being violated, so I made an effigy, a pillow representation of the man, and screamed and punched it until I could feel the anger seeping out of my body and soul. I spoke about it with a therapist, and mourned my lost innocence. I held the little child I used to be, and rocked myself back and forth, telling her that it was okay, that it wasn't her fault. I bought myself a teddy bear, and took it to bed with me at night. I gave myself time to integrate.

Then I tried to imagine what it would have been like to *be* that foster father: how confused and scared and needy he must have been to feel that he could get sexual relief from a nine-year-old child. I experienced a little tinge of sadness for him. I remembered my own fear and pain. And what else? What was my part in it? Did I just happen to be there in that foster home at that time of my life? Was I a victim-in-waiting? Was there something else going on—a lesson for me to learn? I searched myself, and entertained the thought that maybe I too was looking for love, for a father, and perhaps he sensed my need and responded in his own way.

Maybe it was just that I was there and sometimes that's all there is. I could not imagine wanting him to become sexual with me, but I could imagine wanting to be loved, and when I thought about this I began to really understand that

everything we do is a cry for love.

No matter how strange and perverse it may seem, how distorted, crazy or off the mark, most of our actions are cries for love, or what we think of as love. Was my foster father reaching for love by reaching out for me? I choose to think so, and when I think of it that way, I truly can forgive him and let the past go.

I forgive my mates for not living up to the pictures of what I thought they should be. I forgive my children, my brother, my friends, over and over again, for being human, because I have these mental images, these notions in my head of what they should do and how they ought to be! Unless I let go of these and practise forgiveness, I stay stuck.

Look to Yourself

I've gone through my list, and the only person left to forgive is me. Ultimately, I have to forgive myself for believing I was ever supposed to be perfect, or believing that I had the answers for anyone else.

To love yourself is to forgive yourself.

Today I can forgive myself for being enraged in my early life, for not trusting men, for wanting to punish and get back at them. I understand why I hurt the men I was closest to. I can ask their forgiveness and make whatever restitution is possible.

I can ask my children to forgive me for being abusive and neglectful. Today I can be a loving and appreciative mother. Better late than never.

I can ask my friends to forgive me for being self-absorbed. Now I can give friendship back.

When I have forgiven myself and remembered who I am, I will bless everyone and everything I see.[1]

We can only forgive others after we have forgiven ourselves for harboring what we held against them. The sooner we are willing to look at ourselves with compassion, the easier it is to see others that way.

A dear friend turned on me with anger and later called to apologize. I was out so she left a message. *"Can you find it in your heart to forgive me? Will you ever speak to me again?"* Her heart-rending request for forgiveness touched me deeply. There was not a second's hesitation in my picking up the phone. When we hear that call for forgiveness how can we not respond to it?

It's the unforgiving parts of ourselves which we defend against. The more we can accept our own fallibility, the easier this is to do with others. Getting our egos out of the way makes it possible to join with others, and in the joining we are one.

I have read about murder trials where the victims' relatives express forgiveness for the perpetrators and I begin to understand how they could actually accomplish this—how they achieve a greater understanding and thus are able to transform themselves in the process. We can never solve a problem at the level of that problem; we need to shift to a higher level.

I believe that there is "a bit of good in the worst of us, and a bit of bad in the best of us." And who amongst us can judge another's journey? When we forgive ourselves, we let ourselves out of our emotional prisons.

I have had to forgive myself for not being the daughter, sister, mother, wife or friend I wanted myself to be. I must get on with living today and be accountable for what I say and do *now*! I have to forgive every notion of perfection I've held and used a

---

1 *A Course in Miracles* (Penguin Books USA, 1996) at p. 84.

whipping stick to beat myself up with and every projection I've laid upon others as a result of my own inadequacies.

I choose to forgive my mistakes from this perspective: If the great spirit of the universe—my Higher Power—can forgive me, who am I not to? I know I am loved just the way I am. My job is to love me that way too. This is my real work; my task at hand. The extent to which I can do this determines how peaceful and serene I feel inside and creates the quality of my days.

Most days I demonstrate self-forgiveness by living a fulfilled life; by believing I am here on earth to love, to learn, to serve and to grow. My natural state is one of joyous expectancy. When I feel like this, I have an open heart and a ready spirit.

If you long for more joy in your life, you might want to take a look at any grudges you still hold and any people you have not forgiven. If you have shut down any part of yourself by holding onto resentments, you can take big strides on your journey to wholeness through practising forgiveness. You don't have to do it perfectly, either. Just be willing to make a start. You can use the strategies below to heal your heart.

Affirmation: I am willing to forgive myself and others. I am whole and complete.

Celebration Strategies

Finding Forgiveness

Get out a piece of paper and write *"Forgiveness"* at the top of the page. Then ask yourself:

1. Whom do I need to forgive? At whom am I still angry? Whom do I blame?

Write down names and examples. Take your time. Be thorough.

2. Write out your part of the equation.

What was your contribution to each situation?

3. Where do you hold yourself guilty? Where do you feel shame?

4. For what could you forgive yourself?

5. How about the others?

Would you consider forgiving any of them?

6. Start with the easy ones.

Write down the name of the person then write *I forgive you for* _____.

7. Say this aloud a few times.

If there are people you are not yet ready to forgive, could you at least become willing to be willing? How will you accomplish this? Remember, to forgive implies giving. What will you give to yourself, and to others? Will you contact the people you have chosen to forgive, or write them a letter? How will you know you have truly forgiven? What will your payoff be?

Eight

Fulfill Purpose

So many people live as if they're trying to get something, some power stuff, and the "living" part gets diminished. Wake up! I say. This is it! Our purpose is to be, to realize that we are here, to share the newness, to spread the word and deed. Bless circumstances. Bless each day.
Sara Ban Breathnick

We are on a market trip on earth; whether we fill our baskets or not, once the time is up, we go home.
Ibo, Nigeria

We've done a lot of hard work getting to this point. We've been dealing with unfinished business, facing fear, surrendering, analyzing anger, examining expectations, finding forgiveness. Whew! That's a lot. Give yourself a pat on the back or a hug for persevering and congratulate yourself for all the work you've done! Now it is time to focus on going forward and looking at the reason you're alive, your life's purpose. Are you ready?

Have you ever felt as if you are living according to the clock and how much money is in the bank? Have you been driven by time, counting the days and weeks until the holidays, because at holiday time you get away from it all? Are you so accustomed to "doing" that you've forgotten how to "be?" Do you sometimes think life is passing you by? Have you put all your energy into looking after other people's needs? Do you take care of kids and home and spouse—and forget about yourself?

Do you ever feel as if you're losing it? Like you've gone through days, weeks even, in a trance? Do you have a "to-do" list that spills over the edges, and no matter how hard you try, you never come to the end of it? Have you noticed

**there is simply no time for you on your
list or in your life for that matter?**

Your e-mail mushrooms overnight; your cell phone rings more than your land lines although you promised yourself it was just for emergencies. You've got a backlog of mail, meetings to attend, orders to fill, time lines to meet plus family responsibilities and social/community commitments to honor.

Your deeper personal needs are buried by the flurry of outer activities, yet there is a niggling thought at the base of your brain that there's definitely something more, something you've been missing, which you used to know but have forgotten. For a fleeting second the gray matter shifts and there it is, you can almost see it but as you reach out with your mind to grab onto it—it vanishes, leaving you with a vagueness, a sense of discontent, as if you've just missed the boat, but what boat was it?

Stop and Reflect

Do you ever wonder what you're doing here on planet earth; what your real purpose is in life? Are you such a busy person you have no time to look at what that might be?

What is this life if, full of care,
We have no time to stand and stare.

So begins William Henry Davies' poem "Leisure." And what about leisure? Do we really have any? Are we using our leisure time to cram in extra activities? Are we human doings instead of human beings?

Rabbi Zusya, a Hasidic master, once said "If they ask me in the next world, 'Why were you not Moses?' I will know the answer. But if they ask me, 'Why were you not Zusya?' I will have nothing to say."

We each have a purpose in life, a reason for being. It's hard to be true to that purpose if we don't know what it is. One of the ways we stay blind is to keep ourselves very busy, so busy we never have to think about it. Why would we want to avoid our deeper purpose, our inner calling? Perhaps because we think it comes from God and we associate it with pain and suffering. Look what happened to Jesus and Martin Luther King. They heeded the call and got crucified. Yet despite our rushing about, we still have an inkling that we're avoiding something. Even when we don't want to know about God, we do want to believe there is a reason for existence and, in particular, our own existence.

If we believe there is a Divine Force, then it's possible that it is benevolent and wants only the best for us. The best might be fulfilling our destinies: being who we are meant to be, doing work we are passionate about, utilizing our particular talents and living authentically.

Each time I write a book, every time I face that
yellow pad, the challenge is so great. I have written
eleven books, but each time I think, "Uh, oh, they're
going to find out now. I've run a game on every-
body and they're going to find me out."
Maya Angelou

What is this "game" we play, this fear of being found out? I think many of us believe we're not good enough, we don't have the right stuff, so even when we're listening to our inner voice and following our hearts' longing, we feel as though we're pretenders and sooner or later the jig will be up. That's how it is for me. No matter how hard I prepare before giving a presentation, no matter how many glowing evaluations I have stashed away in my files, secretly I think *"This time they'll boo me out of the room."* When I write, the nagging refrain of *"who would ever want to read this stuff?"* admonishes me. Be it presentation jitters or writer's block, I have to push through that nay-saying voice and just go for it.

Find Your Passion

Some of us, like Mozart, are born knowing what our passion—our life purpose—is. Others are groomed for it, like Queen Elizabeth II, John Fitzgerald Kennedy, Martin Luther King, Jacqueline du Pre, Wayne Gretzky, Ben Heppner. Some of us hear the calling of their purpose later in life, like Mother Theresa. Others get it in a blinding flash, like Joan of Arc. Some come to it gradually. What's important is that we do find it, sometimes early in life, sometimes just before we die, but we find it!

Think of that wonderful waitress who makes you feel so at home in your favorite restaurant. Or the librarian who is calm and knowledgeable and has a reverence for reading. Think of the agility of a great basketball player or the trainer of dolphins who communicates in a language only dolphins understand. Isn't it amazing how we find our special niche?

They danced down the streets like dingledodies, and I shambled after as I've been doing all my life after people who interest me, because the only people for me are the mad ones, the ones who are mad to live, mad to talk, mad to be saved, desirous of every-thing at the same time, the ones who never yawn or say a commonplace thing, but burn, burn, burn like fabulous yellow roman candles exploding like spiders across the stars and in the middle you see the blue centerlight pop and everybody goes "awww!"

says Sal Paradise, Jack Kerouac's protagonist in *On The Road*. Sal knew his purpose in life was to follow the people who were interesting to him; it was his passion. Many of us follow the lives of actors and movie stars who explode onto the screen. We're mesmerized and intrigued by them. Do you think we hope a little bit of stardust will rub off on us? Or perhaps some of their passion?

Jeanne Calmet advises us to "[f]ind your passion and explore it with your whole heart and single mind, with your entire being." Each of us has something valuable to share with the world. We don't have to prepare or qualify for our purpose. The fact that we exist means it's within us. Our task is to uncover it. Typically we cover it up *with "shoulds"* or *"ought to's."* Over the years I've listened to many clients saying what they "should" do and I've also heard regret from those who forget to listen to their own direction.

I should go to school and become a doctor even though what I really want to be is a painter but my father expects me to be a doctor because that's what he is. He has a great practice, which he's saving for me and he's already sacrificed so much for my education that I have to become a doctor. Maybe I can paint as a hobby.

Of course, there's never any time to paint, so that dream gradually dies.

I took computer science so I can get a job even though my passion is carpentry and I seem to become attuned to everything when I make furniture.

What I really want to be is a mother and wife. I long to stay home and look after my kids, but I should stay in the workforce because we need the money, although I know we could cut down on our spending and make it work. But if I quit now I might never get another job. There are so many people looking for jobs as it is. I've got a good job; I've worked hard for it. What would I do if I just stayed at home? Let's face it, I'm a liberated women, how can I return to the old paradigm of being just a wife and mother, what would people think?

Do you detect any fear in these statements? Fear pursues us relentlessly, never taking a holiday. When we ignore our destiny and follow someone else's agenda, or use borrowed beliefs about what we should be doing, we sacrifice ourselves.

Sacrifice works for a finite amount of time. Then we need to move on. Another name for sacrifice is being a martyr. When we become martyrs, we end up complaining that we didn't live our lives or follow our dreams *because . . .*

Start Digging

Many of us squander precious natural resources—time, talent and creative energy, comparing ourselves and our talents to others. What a waste! What we need to do instead is go on an inner excavation trip, dig deep, find out what we're here on earth to do. Then do it!

Fulfilling our purpose, finding our passion takes energy and commitment. Friends and family might object or criticize us. But if we don't go for it, our health, happiness, relationships and careers will be adversely affected, and we will miss the point of being here.

My assistant Sue knows what her purpose is. To help others be organized. "My god-given talent is to make life work smoothly for others." When I heard this, I hired her on the spot. Didn't matter that she had no experience in my business and two kids to juggle her job around, she knew what her purpose was and boy did I need her!

Denzell Evans had no clue about his purpose. He ambled along after high school, working in construction, driving a transport truck. When he blinked he was 35 and still didn't know what he wanted to be or do in life. He asked his friends what they thought and they told him he was really good with his hands, so he went to massage school and became a massage therapist for a few years but he got tired of that because what he really wanted to do was help people emotionally. This became his passion. Back to school he went at 50, enrolling in psychology. He took alternative therapy courses on the side. By the time he was 60 he was a practicing therapist, absolutely content, knowing this was his true calling.

Sometimes we think we know what our life purpose is and we pursue that path only to find there is another one beckoning to us.

It takes what it takes.

If we're courageous, we change direction like Cat Stevens did. As a young man Cat Stevens achieved fame as a pop music star. Then, at the height of his career, he followed his inner voice and retreated into a spiritual life. In his 60s poet-musician Leonard Cohen left fame and fortune and moved into a Buddhist monastery. Shirley MacLaine began writing spiritual books after she'd achieved status as an actress.

Because our life expectancy is longer today, many of us have multiple life purposes to fulfill. Gail Sheehy writes about Aaron Coleman Webb:[1]

---

1 *New Passages, Mapping Your Life Across Time* (Toronto: G. Merritt Corp., Random House of Canada Ltd., 1995, at p. 359)

[this man was] virtually canonized as one of the most influential designers of our time, but who had too long used his work to avoid scrutinizing what his life was all about.

It took a heart attack to wake-up Aaron. He and his wife went for a holiday to Tuscany and while there he discovered a little pottery shed, where a father and son sat painting and firing dinner plates. Aaron was fascinated by their simple process, asked if he could come and work with them, and in his sixties, found that he had a new lease on life! He couldn't wait to get up in the morning and drive down to that shed, spending ten hours a day painting plates because he was feeling "deliriously happy." He kept thinking "What is this incredible contentment?" One day he had a flash of insight. "I was doing something I didn't know how to do. And I was learning how to do it!" By peeling back down to the simplest existence and letting himself "play," Aaron rediscovered his greatest joy in life: making things and seeing them transformed into objects of art.

When we lose our sense of purpose it's a pitiful thing. We lose the energy that fuels our spirit and become depleted and disconnected. We search valiantly outside ourselves, looking for something or someone to fill the void and nothing does. When we come to the end of our lives we're apt to say, "Is that all there was?"

No matter how old we are, there is still time and opportunity to fulfill our purpose. All we need to do is look for the opportunities instead of hunting down guarantees. We can take time out and search inside of ourselves. We might discover that what we are doing is exactly what is right for us and we can release any expectations that we should have done anything different. Or we can channel our energy and resources into something new. We can all discover our purpose for we have been given the golden key.

The Golden Key

In the beginning God made man and woman in his image. He wanted to give his master creation every advantage, including the golden key to life. This key held the knowledge that each person has his or her own special purpose for being on earth. God didn't want to make it too easy for us to discover what it was because he knew we'd get bored easily or become complacent. He knew we needed a challenge.

He asked his advisors: "Where shall I put the key to each person's purpose?"

"I think you should put it on top of the highest mountain," one of the wise elders suggested.

"Well that's a good idea," said God nodding his head, "and yet I believe these people are so clever they'll quickly learn how to climb the highest mountain. Let's think of another idea."

"I've got it!" chimed one of his top female advisors. "Let's hide it in the depths of the deepest ocean, they'll never find it there!"

"Great thinking," responded God, "but I suspect they'll learn how to plummet the depths of the deepest water before too long. Still you've given me inspiration. We could hide this knowledge within each person. It will take a long time before they think to look there."

Everybody agreed and the purpose of each life was hidden deep within the soul of every mortal. And it is still so today!

It's helpful to have a mentor or a teacher who can aid us in finding our purpose. George Harrison spent some time with Maharishi Mahesh Yogi in the 1970s, and started playing music in a totally different manner.

Melvin McLeod was a crime reporter who one day opened a book of Buddhist thought and experienced "an instant recognition that that's what I was." Although Melvin continued working as a television reporter, he took a sojourn to India in 1980, looking for a teacher who could "raise the hairs on the back of my neck." His teacher turned out to be Chogyam Trungpa Rinpoche, whose mission was to introduce Tibetan Buddhism to North America. Melvin is now editor-in-chief of the *Shambhala Sun*, a well respected Halifax magazine with a large circulation. His chosen teacher helped him access the world within and he still uses his journalistic talents to make a living based upon his beliefs. With help he actualized his life's purpose.

My client Lisa, a successful lawyer, had a passion for cooking. One day she decided to follow her passion, so she left her job and opened a cooking school. Today she feels like she is living in paradise, doing what she loves and making more money than she did as a lawyer.

Yes, You Can Have It All!

We are all artists—creators of our own life canvas. Some of us are artists in the kitchen, some in the boardrooms, some have a talent for making money, others for making sense. You may not draw, sing, dance or act, but helping a friend through a difficult time is a talent, as is setting an elegant table, creating an atmospheric mood, comforting an aging parent, fixing a computer.

Some of us confuse our purpose with our job. Our job may have nothing to do with our purpose, it may simply be what we do to earn a salary so we can fulfill our purpose. Like Gene, who programs computers yet doesn't derive much satisfaction from his job: "It pays the bills, and it gives me time to do what I really love, coach Little League Baseball."

I watched Gene with his Little League team. Watched him work with those young boys, encouraging them and giving reassurance when they goofed up. I saw the pats on the back and the hugs. Witnessed how he gently modeled caring and team spirit for those little boys. Coaching baseball is Gene's passion and his purpose is to be a loving role model.

Going for our purpose can be demanding. Why am I here? What am I meant to do with my life? How do I find out? What do I actually do when I find out? These questions can challenge us and provoke change. Yet when we find our purpose, we will probably be so excited we'll want to shout it from the rooftops. We'll be on fire with our discovery.

Jacqueline was once a wealthy woman. She owned a successful personal placement agency, a large home, the latest model car and expensive clothes. With all her material wealth, Jacqueline felt empty inside. So she went on a retreat and asked herself life purpose questions. Today Jacqueline feels fulfilled. Although she lives in a modest apartment and walks dogs to make ends meet, Jacqueline knows her purpose is to be of service to others and to express her quirky creativity. She knits teddy bears for children in Romania, makes fabulous meals for her friends, and writes about her tragedies and triumphs to give people hope. She has few pressures in her life and plenty of time to look out the window and dream. Today she measures success by how much love she can give to others, not by how much money she makes.

Our *job* may be what we do to make a living, but our *purpose* is what we do to nourish our spirit.

How many of us live our nightmares, believing we aren't worthy of attaining our dreams? *Life is but a dream*, and we can dream up whatever we want. Follow your dream. Build the baseball field. Actualize! Each one of us has a talent. We need to be still long enough to discover what that is, then align it with our purpose.

Celebration Strategies

Fulfill Your Life Purpose

Gently close your eyes. Breathe deeply, allowing your thoughts to drift by, watching them as if they were clouds floating in the air. When you feel calm and centered, open your eyes, pick up a pen and begin to respond to the following questions.

1. **Which significant events have influenced your life?**

2. **When you were little, what did you love doing MOST?**

3. **How about in high school? What was your passion?**

4. **What do you really like about yourself?**

5. **What interest do you have that you're most afraid of admitting?**

6. **What would you do if you knew you couldn't fail?**

7. **Make a list of 20 things you enjoy.**

Don't think! Give yourself no more than 10 minutes to create this list. Then circle the things that speak loudest to you.

8. **If you were not afraid you would** _____

_____

9. **Affirm.**

"I am willing to live my purpose. My talent at _____
is a blessing for me and for others."

10. Make the commitment to fulfill your purpose whether it's your job or not!

If you have trouble finding your purpose, meander back through your life. Look at photograph albums, read old letters, diaries or journals. What did you once love to do *so much* that time passed away without you noticing it? What did you once enjoy that you no longer do any more? When you search, you will find answers. Use your golden key and unlock your purpose!

St. Francis of Assisi layered the creative process like this: the labor, the craft, the elevation: The person who works only with hands is a laborer; the person who works with hands and head is a craftsperson and the one who works with hands, head and heart is an artist.

It's not *what* we do, it's the *way* that we do it! Many of us have played it safe for too long. We've traded passion for comfort and wonder why we're miserable and unhappy. Playing it safe is the riskiest choice we can ever make. Take a chance and see what happens! You have the golden key; the answers lie within you. All you need to do is ask some questions and listen to your inner guidance.

Do you want to actualize your dreams? Discover your purpose? Access your passion? The time is now!

Affirmation: I am willing to live my purpose. My talent at _____ is a blessing for me and for others.

Nine

Love Ourselves

*The ultimate lesson all of us have to learn
is unconditional love, which includes
not only others but ourselves as well*
Elisabeth Kubler-Ross

To love yourself is to heal yourself
A Course in Miracles

Once I thought love was something to get. Something I needed and could only get from someone else. I wanted it, you had it, and somehow I was going to convince you to give it to me. For a long time I believed unless some man loved me I was incomplete, missing something intrinsic without which I could never be whole, let alone happy. Love was something wiser people had. It was mysterious and elusive. Certainly it kept eluding me. Like a beautiful butterfly, mesmerizing me with its incandescence, love would fly by me, flutter around my heart, then disappear.

Love was desirable yet unobtainable.

It has taken me half a lifetime to solve the mystery and realize that love is something I already have within me. It's both a capacity and an action, which means I can love myself as well as others.

The more I do this, the larger love grows. Loving myself is not a substitute; it's the foundation. Having healthy self-esteem is as vital for my survival as food and water.

Like every baby who comes into the world, I'm sure I started out with plenty of self-regard. Then life happened. When I lost my family and went to live in foster homes, I adopted a shame-based belief system without even knowing it.

My beliefs determined my reality.

I believed my family's breakup was entirely my fault. Believed that I was so bad even my own parents didn't want me.

Our beliefs determine our feelings and our feelings determine our behavior.

Convinced I was bad, I acted out, which in my case took the form of defiance. I hated my name, Jude. It was like a banner, which heralded my shame. On my 13th birthday I changed my name to Angela because there was a popular girl in school whose name was Angela, and my dad had called me his angel.

I buried who I was. Locked up my dishonorable past and became someone else. A girl who spoke up, a woman who looked as if she knew what life was about. It was a sham, I was faking it.

I didn't think I had the goods. I married at a young age because someone who looked worthy wanted me. The belief that I was defective infiltrated that marriage like an uninvited guest who never leaves.

Hurt children grow up to hurt others.

Despite having children and some material security, my self-loathing stayed with me as I traded in that relationship for another. I pretended I was "somebody."

When a person has no genuine self-esteem she feigns it.

I dazzled my new young lover and the act worked for a few years. He was the love magnet, the coveted apple. I thought, *"If I polish this apple, I will get it, this magic thing called love."*

Concentrating on helping him look good and further his career, I lavished all my attention on him, despite the fact that I had three children to raise. Meanwhile, fear wormed its way inside of me. My own self-sabotaging beliefs were steadily eating me up. Thoughts like "what if he finds someone younger, fresher newer? What if he no longer wants the burden of the kids, what if he grows tired of me?" tormented me day and night.

Self is what we bring into relationships. If we lose it, we ourselves become lost. Afraid that he'd leave me, I gave my power to him, put all my love into him. He grew stronger, I got smaller. He flourished, I withered. Finally he left and I suffered. It was only when I hit my emotional bottom, and felt the desperate agony of losing my beloved, that I was willing to even contemplate loving myself. I'd gone through enough failed relationships to know I needed to do something different, even though I didn't know what that would be.

I had discarded me so long ago that I had to travel quite a distance to reclaim who I was. It takes what it takes. We do what we do and get what we get.

Gradually, I began to understand that I had been operating under a misconception. My parents hadn't left because I was bad; they left because of their own turmoil and dysfunction. I had known this truth intellectually, but the subterranean belief, which undermined me, had existed independently and had ruled my life!

Grow Your Love

I decided to grow my own love. Initially this looked like giving up. I gave up my escape through drinking. I gave up smoking. Gave up caffeine, sleeping pills, romance novels, movies and looking for love outside myself. Gave up so much I felt empty. So I started eating. Anything. Constantly. Trying to fill the inner void.

Forty pounds later that craving began to abate as I developed a spiritual appetite. I read books on enlightenment and sampled different spiritual practices, searching for higher wisdom. Simultaneously I was examining my beliefs and becoming aware of the negative messages I was continuously sending myself, messages that robbed me of the quality of life I sought.

"I'm going to be all alone for ever and ever and no one will ever love me," was my recurring self-talk. *"Thanks for sharing but we're doing things differently,"* I'd answer me back, adding a new thought, like: *"I am willing to love and accept myself."*

The hardest thing for me to do was to take care of me, which meant staying with me, going through the panic attacks and the fear voices. Not abandoning or giving up on myself.

By hanging in I began to accept that if there's only me to wake up with in the morning, at least I'm here! I started to feel happy just being alive. This was a big revelation, one that has expanded my life. Today I'd rather be in a healthy relationship with me, than in an unhealthy dependency with anyone else. Today I know I can show up for myself. My most important job on earth is to love me. When I do that, I have something valuable to offer others.

How many of us settle for someone who is not right for us just so we don't have to be alone? How many of us spend our lives knowing we've settled for something that makes us feel angry or frustrated with our choice, but still fearing loneliness?

Positive Self-Talk

I've learned that the biggest loneliness is self-abandonment. Once I seized myself by the hand and reached out for spiritual guidance, I was no longer alone. I brought the name Jude back into my life, and kept Angela too, because she is the me I've forged. Affirmations helped me develop a positive foundation for living. The ones I used initially were:

I, Angela Jude am a radiant child of the universe.

I, Angela Jude, am lovable.

I, Angela Jude, am willing to take good care of myself.

Over and over I'd repeat these affirmations, taking 10 minutes in the morning to write them down, saying each word aloud as I wrote. Filling up notepads. Schooling myself in self-love. Gradually I began to believe what I was writing and whispering to myself.

Whenever I heard my own attack thoughts, I'd substitute a positive phrase. This became a liberating activity. I could see the negative loop my mind played and could instantly change the message. This was quite an achievement!

I began to claim my power, first by going to university at night to get a degree, then by getting a job teaching high school. Later, I left the security of teaching to pursue my dream of being a speaker and author. When I began writing my book, the negative voices rallied. *"Who do you think you are? No one wants to read your book."* I would thank the voices for sharing, and repeat, *"We're doing things differently, I have a message that needs to be heard."* I schooled myself in positive thinking and persevering.

My 13-year-old granddaughter Meiping has a formula for getting through her fear of singing in public. "I can do this," she says to herself, and she says it emphatically, several times, until she believes her own words. Then she opens her mouth and this sweet confident voice emerges. Lately I've been using her system and it works!

All serious daring starts from within.
Eudora Welty

Build Self-Esteem

Self-esteem is like a thermostat, and many of us need to turn it up! Having healthy self-esteem is our birthright. We have healthy self-esteem if we consider ourselves to have worth. We believe we have good qualities and know we make a contribution in life. Healthy self-esteem is a combination of positive beliefs and skills. Accepting our weaknesses is part of self-esteem.

"If you have a weakness that's not important to you, it need not affect your self-esteem," says Ester Cole, president of the Ontario Psychological Association. "If you're a klutz on the squash court but don't particularly value athletic prowess, you can walk away from the court with your self-esteem intact. On the other hand, if you're shy and retiring and wish you were more social, the gap between what you are and what you'd like to be can erode your self-esteem."

When our self-esteem is high, we can weather the storms of life and not feel like we are drowning in them. Recent studies reveal a link between self-esteem and mood disorders. James Battle, a psychotherapist in Edmonton, has studied this link: "There's a striking correlation between low self-esteem and depression." Conversely, high self-esteem goes a long way in orienting us towards a cheerful mood. According to Joanne Wood, a psychology professor at the University of Waterloo "people with low self-esteem may believe that sadness is a part of life and that you shouldn't try to get rid of it, while people with high self-esteem believe in doing something to feel better if they have a negative experience."

Clearly it helps if we start off in life having parents who give us unconditional love. But even when we don't, most of us have had success experiences along the way, and the key to building our self-esteem is to capitalize on these experiences.

Get into the habit of identifying your skills and focus your mind on these areas. Develop new capabilities. Use nurturing self-talk, set and accomplish do-able goals. Mentally re-visit prior successes. By focusing on what's working in our lives, we keep our self-esteem alive and healthy.

Commit to loving yourself.

If you would like to change your life, commit to loving yourself. Make a realistic appraisal of your skills and positive character traits. Set goals—and be aware that as you start to actualize them, your ego mind might step in and try to sabotage your efforts.

Remember EGO is an acronym for Edging Good Out. Our ego mind is our little mind. The part of us that wants us to stay small and secure in our comfort zones, or wallow in familiar self-pity. We have a larger mind that is always available. We can access it by calling on our Higher Power to guide us. We can transcend self-doubts and negative behavior patterns.

Fear has destroyed more dreams than we can ever know. Physical distress—a racing heart, sweating palms, pounding head, nervous stomach, shaking hands, an overwhelming desire to sleep, those are our first physical assaults when we creep to the edge of our comfort zone. But keep going. Even though it may feel scary making that telephone call, speaking up during a meeting, or dropping off your résumé to a prospective employer, keep going! Remember you are only leaving your comfort zone, not your life. Calmly reassure yourself that the feeling of fear is passing through you and will dissipate as long as you keep moving forward. Many performers are terrified each time they approach an audience, however they've learned to transform fear into creative energy. So can you.

When you hear fear whisper *"Who do you think you are? You can't do this, you don't have the training, you'll make a fool of yourself if you do this,"* or when you hear the calmly lethal voice of procrastination by intimidation saying: *"I don't want to alarm you, but you've taken on quite a lot. I wouldn't do this if I were you, at least not now. Wait a while, you've got plenty of time, there's always tomorrow,"* immediately silence these voices. Say *"cancel, cancel"* or *"thanks for sharing,"* then put a new thought in place. Know that moving out of your comfort zone feels yucky, but it is only a feeling. Play some gorgeous music to drown out those voices. Dance yourself through fear, prance through intimidation. Open wide the doors to your limitless being. Boldly stride through patterns of self-sabotage. Visualize success.

You can do it, I know you can. You can do it because I did it so you can too. You are worth it. The life you consciously create for yourself is beyond anything you can imagine now. And it's waiting for you.

Today I know that

love really is an action word

and *I* need to take the action. Starting with taking care of me. I no longer think of loving me as selfish but as necessary. Even the Bible teaches love thy neighbor *as thyself!*

I still struggle with being able to hold my own when I feel criticized. One night I showed my 10-minute promotional video to my brother Nick and his partner, Hara, who were visiting for a couple of weeks. At the end of the video there was a big silence. My self-esteem started sliding.

Hara began questioning me: "Why do people just do what you say? Why do they listen to you?"

Gulp. I started turning red, at least on the inside.

Then Nick jumped in, "Why do they hire you? I mean, what is it they expect to gain?"

I tried answering him, but I could feel the defensive anger beginning to rise in me at the same rate as confidence was ebbing away.

"I've been working for a company for 20 years and we've never had anything like this," he added, shaking his head.

Ouch. From an outer corner of my mind I remembered an affirmation I'd learned and had used many times when I was working hard at building my confidence. *"No matter what you say and do I'm still a worthwhile person."* I began repeating this sentence to myself, over and over. It calmed me down and gave me a minute to think, time to quell the desire to strike back with words. Getting up from the couch, I went to the bathroom to give myself space, and as it was late at night, excused myself and went to bed.

Sometimes distance is an appropriate antidote.

During the night I wrestled with thoughts of revenge, like punishing them both by withholding my presence. I contemplated escape. At the same time, my saner self was telling me that they were both from a different country, from a different world in fact, and knew nothing about what I did for a living, so why be upset? What I needed was to understand their perspective without losing my own. If I could do that, then I would be okay no matter what they said or did.

In the morning I did my yoga stretches and prayed for help. It came as I read a passage in my meditation book, which reminded me that whenever I hold a grievance against someone else, I cut myself off from the light. I love living in the light, so I reached out for it again. Forgave my interpretation of their actions and simply let it go.

Walking back inside the cottage I smelled the early morning coffee, the enticing aroma of breakfast being cooked. Smiles, good mornings, a yummy breakfast followed by a good talk. No one was damaged, there was no unfinished business. This was a far cry from my past behavior of sulking, spewing or holding resentments.

One of the advantages of aging is being able to do things differently. Some of us accumulate wisdom by default. Others have to work hard at it. We all get plenty of opportunities to practice!

People are put in our paths for us to interact with: grocery clerks, bank tellers, neighbors, people passing by to smile at. The more love we give, the more comes back to us.

Love, I've discovered, doesn't run out. It has no beginning or end. Love is always available; it's eternal and infinite. I can't buy it, own it or keep it. I can make it, grow it, nurture it, delight in it and offer it to others. My daughter Tanya says

love is like a knitted scarf.

There are rows of family love, rows of friendships, work, support groups, acquaintances, community, the world at large, and the entire scarf is nothing but rows connected by love!

When I don't love myself, I fall back into childish behavior. I want you to love me instead. I want you to do it for me and give it to me. Don't get me wrong, I like being on the receiving end, feeling adored, being heard, getting stroked. Yet I know that love lies within me. It's my well, and I have to continuously prime the pump.

Sometimes love means saying "No" to habits that don't nourish us or to people who are demeaning. Saying "No" to taking on too much, or to doing things that are not in sync with who we are; to borrowed beliefs; to pleasing and appeasing in the hope of getting love.

When we say "No" we must then learn to close our mouths. No excuses or apologies. This may anger some folks who are used to our "yeses" but that's their business to work out, not ours.

Being authentically you may cost you. You may even have to let go of certain friends or relationships; people who want you to stay the way you were. This can be painful, but I want you to remember,

when one door closes another opens,
even though it is hell in the hallway.

Despite the uncertainty of walking through the hallway of transition, you can be sure that there are doors in this hallway that will gradually open. New people will be attracted to you and these people will reflect your authentic self. When you are a whole person you attract others who are whole as well. When you're a friend to yourself, your friendships are healthy.

Friendship with oneself is all important
because without it one can not be friends
with anyone else in this world
Eleanor Roosevelt

It may happen that being your authentic self means saying goodbye to the person you were supposed to be so you can become the person you want to be.

You can give yourself a regular congruency check to see if you've said anything or done anything that is not in line with who you are. Notice if you abandon yourself by smiling when you are angry, or attacking someone else to cover up your hurt. Observe when you agree to something that does not sit well with you. You can always backtrack and change your decision.

When you find you're acting unkindly to yourself, say you're sorry and give yourself a hug. Know that you can take tiny steps instead of giant leaps. Remember that there's always another opportunity waiting in the wings.

Loving you means creating time to be alone in.

Take time to grow your love.

I treasure my alone time. I need it every day. This is not a luxury, it's a necessity.

Giving myself time to do spiritual practices in the morning starts my day on a positive note. Giving myself permission to go slower in life, instead of feeling like I have to race through my days, keeps me relaxed. Listening and acting on my inner voice is a way of treating myself with respect. The most precious gift you can give yourself is the gift of time.

As Gladys Taber says: "We need time to dream, time to remember, and time to reach the infinite. Time to be."

Here are some other ideas that are helpful for increasing our love.

Celebration Strategies

Loving Ourselves

1. Build your love bank.
Think about someone who believed in you. Who cared enough about you to encourage you. What did this person say or do? Take some time to reflect. Could you give this same encouragement to yourself when you need it? What would you say?

2. Use affirmations.
If you are someone who has a hard time taking time just for you, then try this affirmation:

I _____ *[state your name] am now willing to make time for myself.*

Write this affirmation in your best handwriting, repeating each word to your self. Write it out 10 times a day for a minimum of 30 days. Repeat it to yourself whenever you can. The more you work your affirmation, the more it works for you.

3. Demonstrate your love.

How do you demonstrate self-value? What loving action can you take today? Will you make time for simple pleasures, like reading a book, or walking in some fresh air? Can you make a commitment to eat well and get the rest you need? Will you give yourself time to do nothing in? A simple gesture can be the beginning of a lifelong habit of self-love. What will you start with?

4. Ask a friend.

Ask a good friend to write out an advertisement for you, as if you were placing it in the newspaper. At the same time write your own ad. Which one is better? Read the ad every day.

5. Go for it!

Choose an activity you love to do and perhaps haven't done for a while. Or choose one you have never done at all, and go for it. It might be scuba diving, ballroom dancing or visiting a museum. Perhaps you love to work with your hands—needlepoint, calligraphy, bookbinding, gardening, framing pictures, creating sculptures. Give your imagination free reign then get active.

Need more help? Here are a few suggestions:
- Take sailing or fencing lessons
- Learn a new language
- Sign up for a painting class
- Join a fitness club

- Book a weekly massage
- Enroll in a book club
- Sit quietly and do nothing

6. Laugh frequently.

Especially when you make mistakes. Mistakes are a sign of growth. Remember, you are here to learn, not to be perfect!

7. Whisper love words.

Whisper love words to yourself regularly. Encourage yourself; give yourself hugs.

8. Treat yourself like royalty.

Every so often, treat your self to a gourmet dinner or a magnificent opera, concert or play. Buy a brand new hardcover book. Indulge in a day at the spa. Order new golf clubs. Reserve the best seats at the ballgame.

Creating authentic self-worth is love in action. Enjoy loving you!

Affirmation: I love myself and take good care of myself

Ten

Love Others

In a real sense all life is interrelated.
We're all caught in a single garnet of destiny.
I can never be what I ought to be until
you are what you ought to be.
Martin Luther King

All that is necessary to make this world
a better place to live is to love—to love
as Christ loved, as Buddha loved.
Isadora Duncan

Love is the mortar that holds the human struc-
ture together. As such, we need to spend our
time, our money, and our inspiration on loving
others. On loving them as they are, because when
we do that we all reap the rewards. It is
important to realize that you cannot accept
any more love than you are willing to give.
Amrit Desai

I think love is our home. It's the place we are coming from, the moving river of life that flows within us, and the place we are going to. Let's face it, we are either loving or we are not. If we love, people are attracted to our energy and appear in our lives so we can love them and be loved by them.

To be loved unconditionally is our birthright, however, many of us did not receive this kind of love as children. We look for approval from others and we search intently for signs of love before giving it. Many of us are searching rather than loving. We've forgotten that we need to first give what we want to receive.

> ***If you would be loved, love, and be loveable.***
> Benjamin Franklin

As I understand it, loving unconditionally means letting go of all expectations. It means full acceptance of someone else, the good, the bad and the ugly. Not easy, but immensely rewarding.

> ***The greatest thing,***
> ***you'll ever learn***
> ***is just to love***
> ***and be loved in return . . .***
> *Nature Boy* by Eben Ahbez

How I loved to hear my father's resonant deep voice gently cascading over these words as he sang *Nature Boy*. It seemed to me that this song came from his feet and moved all the way up through his body. I caught the yearning, carried it around in me, and made it my life's purpose. Eventually the yearning got replaced by learning, and I am still a novice when it comes to love.

Change Your Restaurant, not Your Relationship!

Why is loving so difficult? It sounds easy, doesn't it? All we have to do is . . . *do it!*

Well if it was that easy, we'd all be doing it! I believe that loving others, *really* being able to love another person, is the hardest work we ever do. In North America, our staggering separation and divorce rates attest to how challenging it is to hang in when the going gets rough. It is much easier to start over again with a "fresh" person. I'm a casualty of this kind of thinking, and what I've learned is that it might save us a lot of heartache and alimony if, instead of travelling from one person to another, looking for the perfect mate, we had a "fresh" look at our own expectations and shortcomings.

If it is variety we crave, we could change our restaurants instead of our relationships.

Loving others is our individual and universal quest, our holy grail. We need to keep first things first and remember what we came here for, what our common purpose is. It's not about adding more to our busy life. It is about taking away what we've used to cover up our love. Releasing those tight lips and harsh judgments. Letting go of whatever we use to hold back our love.

Typically we create reasons to keep ourselves emotionally separate from one another. Reasons like "I'd love him more *if* . . . he put his things away . . . if he was more romantic . . . if he did what I asked him to" or "I'd love her more *if* . . . she stopped telling me what to do . . . if she didn't talk so much . . . if she was more sexy." Each of us has reasons for withholding affection and stopping the river of love from flowing in our hearts. The problem is, we actually listen to our own head noise and let these limiting beliefs and negative scripts run our lives.

What would your life look like if you loved your partner unconditionally? If you accepted him/her *exactly* as he/she is? Without lecturing, scolding or trying to improve a thing? What would be different?

Do you remember when you first met your beloved? Do you recall the fluttering in your heart, how you had difficulty sleeping or eating, how loud your own swallowing sounded because you were so conscious of being close? Can you bring to mind the excitement that permeated your entire being, how you had to talk with or hopefully see your loved one as often as possible, just to feel alive?

Then you started living together or got married and what happened?

I can tell you what happened for me. I did what I'd vowed I'd never do, took him for granted. Accepted the roses he brought me, then later began to wish he'd show more imagination and buy a different flower. I nagged, just like my mother. When he came home, the first thing I'd notice was his gut, leading the way.

I'd watch how much butter he'd spread on his bread, how often he'd eat ice cream, how much cream he'd put in his coffee, and I wanted him to stop because . . . *I'd love you if!* I ceased listening to him because I already knew what he was going to say. Instead I offered advice, pointing out what he should have done. Then I blamed him because I'd lost that loving feeling. Told him I was fantasizing about other men and it was his fault because he wasn't romantic enough, he wasn't giving me what I needed. I projected my feelings of separation onto him.

"I'd love him if . . . he'd do what I want him to do, be how I want him to be." Do you know what I'm talking about?

Often we swing between two poles in life, the push/pull extremes. When we're alone we want to be with someone, when we're with someone we want more space. With patience and hard work we can create a healthy balance of being with others and being alone. We don't have to start fights to get that space either. We can simply acknowledge that we need it.

Years ago my mother-in-law told me that she spent 75% of her free time away from her husband and I was shocked. I thought it meant she didn't love him very much and I vowed never to let that happen to me. But you know, lately I've realized that I spend about 60% of my time away from my husband because I need that time for me! And it makes the time when we're together more special.

Carly, 42

Like Carly, I've discovered that loving my partner means having time apart, so we will individually grow and have more to offer one another. When we first got together, Fraser and I were inseparable, which of course is natural in a new relationship. Because both of us had been in previous relationships, we knew we had to keep our individual interests alive, yet it was challenging to move out of our "cocoon" phase. Today I can tell you that I'm grateful we did. What I've learned is that those times apart keep the relationship healthy.

Often I take time to be with my women friends and I also take holidays on my own during the summer months. Fraser facilitates men's workshops, spends time with his friends and goes to retreats on his own. We have individual friendships and separate interests in addition to the interests we pursue together, and I believe this keeps our relationship "green and growing" rather than "ripe and rotting."

Banishing the Inner Critic

When I hear my judgmental mind starting to find fault with anyone, I try to use it as an opportunity to develop more tolerance. I've discovered that my attempts at correcting someone are a complete waste of time, so I banish the inner critic and look for good qualities instead.

The only way I've been able to stop projecting negativity outwards is to realize that all fault finding is really about me. This is hard work. It's much easier to point the finger at him. When I hear my critical voice I swivel the fault finding telescope towards me. Truth is, I have to change my perceptions and accept him or her as is, no conditions. That's where the growth is.

Lonnie, a client, calls our faults "blemishes." I like that, it's a polite way of addressing our flaws.

I've accepted that it's really not my job to improve anyone except myself and when I fall back into old habits, I reach for my "Prescription for Loving" and apply one or two doses. This practice works whether it's being used on my family, friends or colleagues. A great example of love in action came from Mother Teresa. Leaving her convent school in Calcutta she took her ministry to the slums, working on the streets with the sick and dying, amidst squalor, disease and poverty. No one was turned away. What a magnificent legacy of love she gave us.

Sometimes it's easier to feel affection for strangers than it is to love family. Because family know us, they see our foibles and even talk about them. Then we get mad and return the favour. Point out their faults. Play tit for tat, becoming defensive.

> *A person needs to be loved the most*
> *when he deserves it the least.*
> John Maxwell

Have you noticed that it's really hard to love others when they're in an "ugly" state? The remedy is to look at the person *as if* we loved them unconditionally. And sometimes we just need to get out of their way.

First Do No Harm

The longer I live, the more I'm convinced that being kind to others, releasing expectations and listening without offering advice, is how we best demonstrate love. And it's a choice, isn't it? Every day we can choose to love, choose to be happy. We don't even have to go to anywhere; we can begin right in our own hearts and practise in our homes.

Families are spiritual workouts.

They strengthen our emotional muscles. When family is around, I get to witness my behavior. To notice how I fall into traps, how although I say choose happiness, I also choose to abandon it at the first sign of trouble. Knowing my pattern makes it easier for me to shift when I catch myself repeating it. Plus, I have incentive. If I don't do the work, I'll go through more pain.

Praise softens. Criticism hardens. Many of us seek love and claim we can't find it. Love comes to us because it is attracted to itself. When I'm bothered by something he or she does, I say *"HIII"* out loud. HIII stands for *"How Important Is It?"* In the grand scheme of things, what I'm upset about is usually not significant.

When he arrives all crabby and shaggy, I make myself look at him with eyes of love. As if he's movie star stunning. Gradually I begin to see the light in him start to glow again. When she gets snippy and makes those nasty digs, I concentrate on remembering that there is only fear and love, so she must be feeling a lot of fear. Then my heart opens and compassion flows.

Only connect! Only connect and human love will be
seen at its height. Live in fragments no longer.
Only connect, and the . . . isolation that
is life . . .will die.
E.M. Forster

Our Children Are Our Teachers

Everywhere we go we have connection opportunities. Each person we encounter is our teacher. Children are particularly fine teachers because they live in the moment and are honest.

My granddaughter Meiping is one of my best teachers. I learned an invaluable lesson from her one March, when she was seven years old. We were walking on a beautiful white sandy Florida beach one sunlit morning. She was picking up shells and running back to me to show me her treasures. Impatiently I looked at these shells, wanting to say: "Meiping, put those shells back because they're all broken. Wait until you find the perfect shells," but for some reason I said nothing and listened to my words forming. With a jolt I realized I was applying grown-up standards to a child. Which started me thinking about grown-up standards and what this mania for perfection was really about. Joining her search, I bent down and started picking up broken shells and discovered that no matter how chipped or broken each shell was, there was something of beauty in each one. It might be the color, or the shape, or the lines or indentations, but the beauty was there, just because the shell was there.

Now I apply this metaphor to people, and I often carry a chipped shell with me, so I can remind myself that we all have chips and blemishes and there is no such thing as perfection. Which doesn't mean I don't want to improve. It just means I accept my own humanity more. Therefore I can accept yours.

Life just keeps on presenting those growth opportunities. Robert Frost put it succinctly: "Our very life depends on everything's recurring till we answer from within." And from Rumi, the great Persian poet: "Everything in the universe is within you. Ask all from yourself." If you want more love in your life, be more loving. Pick up a shell, or a stone, and carry it with you as a talisman.

Make time for people in your life. Contact those you love and tell them. Cultivate friendships by being a friend. Stay connected with family. Pay less attention to the paycheque or promotion and more attention to the twinkle in those old eyes, or the tottering steps of a baby.

An Egyptian myth says that when we die, our heart is cut out of our body and placed on a scale. If our heart weighs more than a feather, it is thrown to wild animals, but if it weighs less, then we live in paradise because we've given our love away.

> *The love in your heart wasn't put there to stay,*
> *Love isn't love 'till we give it away.*
>
> Anon

Tony, a colleague, shared his guideline for relationships with me:

- See everything
- Learn something
- Overlook lots

What profound wisdom!

For those of you who enjoy gardening, I've adapted some hints on loving from D.J. Harrington's *Garden for Success*:[1]

First plant three rows of "peas":

- Patience
- Perseverance
- Positive Action

---

1 D.J. Harrington is a well-known author, journalist and trainer. You can see more of his garden at http://www.djharrington.com/garden.php.

Then plant four rows of "squash":

- Squash indifference
- Squash negativity
- Squash worry
- Squash envy

Next plant five rows of "turnips":

- Turn-up with a smile
- Turn-up with new ideas
- Turn-up with warmth
- Turn-up on time
- Turn-up with determination to put your best foot forward

No garden is complete without "lettuce":

- Let us be honest with each other
- Let us meet our goals
- Let us forgive one another
- Let us play and have fun together
- Let us love and help one another

Take care of one another.

Last summer Fraser and I went to Scotland to trace his roots, and although we didn't come up with too much in the way of ancestry, we met some delightful people on our journey and I fondly remember dear Mrs. MacPherson, smiling broadly at us and saying "take care of one another," as she waved farewell.

It's so easy to write about love and so challenging to keep on loving, especially when we feel inadequate or irritated with the person we're supposed to be loving. Ultimately we need to be patient with ourselves when we miss our mark, and realize that we have many more opportunities ahead to get better at it.

Celebration Strategies

Prescription for Loving

Here is my prescription for loving. You might want to keep this someplace where you can easily see it. When you find yourself being critical of someone, apply the prescription.

It comes in five doses.

1. There is only fear and love.

2. This is an opportunity to practise loving.

3. How would I behave if I loved him or her unconditionally?

4. Criticism doesn't change a thing. Never fear the worst in people and concentrate on their best.

5. When you get into an argument, ask yourself "Will I put my energy into connection or separation?"

Affirmation: I am willing to be loving

Eleven

Live Healthy

Better keep yourself clean and bright;
you are the window through
which you must see the world.
George Bernard Shaw

Do the thing you think you can not do!
Eleanor Roosevelt

Habits are easier to change if you are
dedicated to taking small steps consistently,
while never losing sight of the goal.
Rob Sugar, weight-loss coach

L iving healthy sounds good, and most of us know it's the way
we were meant to live.
So why don't we?

"I eat well all day, but when night comes and I'm lonely, I stuff
myself with junk food."

Moira, 36.

"I can't tell you how many times I've joined a health club and
exercised faithfully for two or three months. Then something

happens: my schedule at work gets changed, or I become too busy, so I start missing classes and before I know it, months pass and I've gained weight, spent all this money and now I've got to start all over again.

Adrianne, 45.

"I know I'm living on adrenaline, but I'm building my future. I have two kids and a wife to take care of. I work 16-hour days. Maybe later, when I'm older, I'll be able to slow down."

Ron, 32.

When I think about living healthy, I think of feeling emotionally centered yet having a sense of exhilaration, an expectancy of spirit, matched with strength and endurance in my body, and clarity in my mind. Body, mind, spirit and emotions—I need all four in good working order to have "zest in my step, zing when I sing."

A healthy body is a happy body, and a happy body is cared for. Simply put, it gets enough food, exercise, inspiration, sleep and play to keep it tuned up and conditioned. So why do some of us ignore our bodies and reside only in the mind? Why do we have people struggling with obesity or anorexia? Why do we compulsively exercise, subjecting our bodies into an idealized image of what we think we should look like? Or, conversely, why do we give up on us and become lethargic couch potatoes? Why do we walk around disappointed with the bodies we've been given? Why are we fixated on looking youthful? What does this say about our values? Asking questions can help us get clearer, even if we don't have any answers.

A native proverb says each of us is a house with four rooms physical, mental, emotional, mental, and spiritual. Many of us live in one or two of our rooms, yet to have a healthy life we need to spend time in each of these rooms.

Imagine owning a beautiful house
but only living in part of it!

In our spiritual room we need to connect with our deeper
selves, in our emotional room we need to be aware of and express
our feelings, in our mental room we need to keep our minds agile,
and in our physical room we need food, exercise and sleep. Let's
start the tour of our house in our physical room.

Eating Right

It's my taste buds and my mind that get me in trouble!

I don't know about your body, but my body knows when it's
eating well. It thrives on vegetables, fruit, grains and protein. It's
my taste buds and my mind that get me into trouble.

My taste buds crave chocolate, coffee, cream, cheese, cookies,
chips, nuts and bread lathered with butter. My mind wants more
of everything. So I fluctuate between eating healthily and deca-
dently.

I've tried to eat only what's good for me, and that works for a
while, but then I fall into indulgent ways again. I've gone off sugar,
flour, salt and caffeine only to end up obsessing about key lime pie
and cappuccinos with chocolate sprinkles.

In high school we read James Hilton's *Lost Horizon*, a gem of
a book that stressed moderation. The notion of moderation has
plagued me, because I tend to be immoderate, so I play with it. For
example, I'll make sure I have greens, grains and proteins for
dinner and then I'll eat ice cream for dessert. Or I'll go without
dessert and enjoy some wonderful foccaccia bread. Or I'll have
apples for a snack one day and chocolate the next.

Deprivation doesn't work for me. I've tried fasting only to end
up over-indulging later. So now I experiment with combining what
I drool over and what I know is good for my body. The secret of my

success is that I don't give myself a hard time when I indulge and I think I'm eating well.

The power is in the word *think*. Remember what Henry Ford said? "Whether you think you can, or you think you can't, you're right!" If we think we care for our bodies, we will.

Like gasoline for our cars, food fuels our bodies. Good fuel = a smoothly running body. Unlike gasoline, we are constantly bombarded with articles about which food is good for us. One month butter is in, the next month it's margarine. Should we eat meat or poultry? Fish is good for us but what about the mercury factor? We have the Low Fat diet, the Carbo Addicts diet, the Atkins diet, the Fit for Life diet, but where is the Love Yourself while you Eat diet? And speaking of diets, do you realize that the first three letters in diet spell die? Do we die from our diets?

Millions of people battle with weight problems and billions of dollars are spent on books and exercise equipment. I would not presume to tell anyone what to eat, for what is right for each one of us is a purely personal matter. Besides which, most of us know we have to pay attention to our cholesterol count and caloric intake. Still, we sabotage our best intentions. And why? Perhaps because we're hungry on a deeper level. We use food as a soother, a panacea. Instead of feeling our loneliness or anxiety, we gulp, chomp and chew our emotions down, setting up food dependency in the process. Our stomachs get larger, we have to fill them up to feel whole, and the vicious cycle becomes entrenched. Do you think it's time we asked ourselves why we eat too much or not enough? Could we make a decision to tend to our deeper needs and learn to eat with love?

When I discovered that I used food to fill up an inner emptiness, I made a decision to stay conscious as often as possible and feel what was going on inside, instead of ransacking the refrigerator for my next fix. That simple decision has made a huge difference in my life. I now know that it is possible to alter our relationship with food so that we feel nourished instead of stuffed.

Here are some suggestions for encouraging healthy eating.

- **Use food preparation as a meditation**
Become calm *before* taking anything out of the fridge. Breathe tranquility into your body, and exhale tension.

- **Stay present**
Enjoy each moment of preparation. Watch how the water sparkles when washing lettuce. Marvel at the bright orange color of carrots and the brilliant iridescence of fish.

- **Find healthy alternatives**
If you tend to use fast food or whatever is on hand when you're hungry, do a little planning to protect yourself. Keep a bowl of fruit handy and stock your freezer with healthy options.

   Order home cooked meals carefully made by someone else, and have them easily available. There are several companies who do this listed in the Yellow Pages and on the Internet. You could also put up a sign at your local health food store and see what responses you get.

- **Practice diligence**
Love your body enough to read the small print on packages and cans. Then you can decide if you want to ingest those chemicals. Schedule enough time for good food selection. Organic produce has found its way to most supermarkets, and we have natural food shops to support us. When we concentrate on loving our bodies, we'll choose our fuel well.

   Especially if you eat alone, you need to enhance your mealtimes. Put a flower or a candle on your table. Play some peaceful music and savor each bite of food. Chew! Put down the book, turn off the television, and take sensual pleasure from eating. As for those busy dinner times when noisy children seem to rule and the whole meal is over in minutes, here are a couple of options: Have family nights and parent nights. Declare special dinner times for adults, with no interruptions, and yes, they can watch their favorite DVDs while you enjoy your privacy, or let the kids eat first and adults later.

Get help if you need it.

If you're ignoring or obsessing about food, you can get help from a physician or nutritionist. Enroll in a weight control program. Take cooking classes to become more creative. Join a self-help group to deal with food compulsions. When we establish a loving relationship with our bodies, then eating in a healthy manner becomes automatic.

Exercise for Fun

It's how we exercise that counts!
As for exercise, there is a smorgasbord to pick from. Walk, jog, dance, swim, roller blade, in-line skate, hike, bike, skate, ski, play racquet sports or team sports; they are all available. The key is to choose what you enjoy.

My friend Lee is a runner. Every morning she's up at dawn, running with a group of friends. My brother Nick runs marathons. A friend in-line skates, one of my daughters bikes, the other goes to a fitness club, my son plays hockey and I take dance classes. Each of us does what we like best with varying intensity. I hear the refrain:

"it's not what you do, it's the way that you do it"

as I write, and I'm reminded that it's how we exercise that counts. Make exercise fun, and you'll stay motivated.

Sleep Well

Many of us have sleep concerns. We go full tilt all day long then fall exhausted into bed only to wake up a few hours later, anxious about what we did or did not accomplish. We fret about yesterday and worry about tomorrow. Sleep clinics, pharmaceutical companies and psychologists are benefiting from our sleep disorders, and I think we can take charge of our sleep by managing our lives better.

We could start by becoming satisfied with whom we are, and what we do, period.

We could gear down before getting into bed.

Sit quietly and watch a flickering candle flame. Read something calming. Have a warm bath. Listen to relaxing CDs. These are some of my favorite wind-down practices and you undoubtedly have others you like. The key here is consistency. Below are some other ideas for healthy sleeping:

- Create a bedroom that is calming
- Eliminate clutter
- Buy cotton sheets so your skin can breathe
- Invest in an air filter
- Get a massage
- Use a humidifier during winter months
- Try a white noise machine if you need to drown out sounds

The main thing is to keep the main thing the main thing. Love your body enough to help it relax.

Visit Your Emotional Room

I've talked about emotions throughout this book, but what I haven't discussed is the therapeutic power of laughter and play.

Do you remember being young and yearning to go out and play? What I recall is that there never seemed to be enough hours in the day to have all the fun I wanted. There were games to discover, imaginary houses to fix up, pictures to color, scary stories to hear, bikes to ride, skates to roll on, marbles to pocket, places to investigate, the list was endless.

We need to make time to play!

Do you let yourself out to play? I'm not talking about exercise classes or sewing circles. I mean silly-goofy-fooling-around-can't-wait-to-get-at-it playing. Just having fun. Playing is vital in our busy lives. We need to make time for it and schedule it in our agendas with colored markers.

While visiting Florida, I was amazed by the amount of playing those senior citizens did. They attended creative workshops, painted, biked, played tennis, swam, read, danced and acted in non-professional theatre. They took trips, played cards, fished, curled, bowled, walked the beach and entertained. At the opera I noticed one fine fellow sitting with two stuffed teddies on his lap. The older folks seemed to know that the secret of life is to celebrate it every day. I was envious so I signed up for jazz dancing.

It takes one a long time to become young
Pablo Picasso

Playing is good for our health and laughter is a great stress reliever. We don't need any special equipment to laugh or any reason. All we have to do is take a look in the mirror! Or kick-start the automatic laugh mechanism by saying "hahahahaha" over and over again.

I've read that kids laugh about 100 times a day. Lately I've been selecting funny movies and I can tell you it's helping me to get my daily laugh quotient. I also read the comics and watch people, particularly at airports. You can see the whole spectrum of human drama at an airport; grandpas nuzzling babies, mothers coping with kids, dads juggling luggage, lovers embracing—tears, hugs, smiles and plenty to chuckle about.

Earlier today my friend Denise called. "I've had tons of visitors this past month, my house has been heavy with traffic, now they've all gone and I just want to scream," she said.

We talked and laughed together, commiserating over the guests we've had, the one that had to plan everything around taking vitamins every two hours and the one who had an exercise routine so regimented she insisted on biking even when there was thunder and lightning. The one who shopped for the entire week and had to ship cartons of purchases home, all the while complaining about her too-crammed apartment. Yes, we loved having our guests, and it was wonderful to notice their idiosyncrasies. Because we're human.

Last Saturday I'd invited guests for dinner. Being a nervous cook, I planned an Italian menu, because lasagna and caesar salad I can do! At 5 P.M. I realized I'd forgotten the bread and romano cheese, so I jumped into my car and sped to the nearby supermarket.

Making my way through the parking lot I looked in the grocery store windows and saw the most handsome young man I had seen in years standing at the check-out counter.

Mr. Gorgeous! And he was looking right at me. Figuring it was because I was wearing a fuchsia pantsuit, and was hard to miss, I nonetheless straightened my shoulders as I entered the store. Quickly picking out my items, I sashayed to the check-out counter, casually glancing his way. Yes, he was still there and now he was staring at me! Fluffing my hair, I thought: "This young man obviously has very good taste. He knows older women are more sophisticated, more sensitive." So caught up in my thoughts was I, that when the cashier gave me my change, I dropped it. Reaching down to pick it up I noticed there was a long white piece of toilet paper hanging from the waistband of my fuchsia pants.

That's why he'd been staring at me!

For an instant I felt mortified, but I found myself winking at him as he passed me by, and I smiled all the way home. That night I told my guests about it and we ended up trading embarrassing experiences. I laughed until tears ran down my cheeks and I nearly fell off my chair.

Thank goodness for laughter. It's a great tonic and so good for us. Our heart gets a workout, the muscles in our face get toned, our skin glows, our circulation gets stimulated, and we release endorphins, nature's "happy hormones."

Laughing increases our face value.

When we laugh we feel as if we're on top of the world, and can do anything. And laughing sooner is better than later, but later is better than not at all. How many times have you said "Someday I'll look back and laugh about this?" Someday is now!

There are times when I've lost my laughter; times I've been embroiled in emotions or faultfinding. Painful times, stressful times. Times when laughter seems far away, almost like a foreign country. I've had to make a special effort to bring it back into my life again. Here's what I use:

- reading funny stories, comic strips, watching silly movies
- sharing embarrassing moments, big mistakes
- visiting my grandchildren
- going to a comedy club with a friend
- getting on my bicycle, pretending it's a horse, and riding with the wind
- going for a swing at the park
- dancing alone to wild music
- doodling with scented markers

When the moon is full and you get caught in one of those "no-sleepers" you could get up and dance, or listen to the birds' serenade.

When was the last time you took a moonlit walk?

Could you play with your shadow? Howl with the dogs? Let the magic incandescence of moon glow capture your imagination and see where it leads you.

There's an innocence within each one of us that knows how to be in the moment; how to live life fully and hold time lightly. To enjoy a sunset without having to own it. To let ice cream dribble down our chins. When I give myself permission to play, it's like opening a toy box.

I start doing one thing, like dancing, then I call a friend who has a wicked sense of humor and before I know it, I feel equipped to handle anything.

Work with heart

Let's look at our work environment. Do you ever feel that work and play are mutually exclusive? Too often I become so embroiled in my work that every thing seems urgent and serious and I end up stressing myself. When I learned that surgeons often operate with rock music booming around them, I decided to see if I could merge work and play, and cut down on the physical tension. Now I have music playing softly in the background while preparing presentations, I read newspaper comics for smiles, and every hour or so I move my body and some-times break out into a one-minute dance.

Work and play belong together!

Since adopting these practices I feel more relaxed and happy by the end of the day.

I think it is easy to get caught up in the pressures of the moment and lose sight of what's important. We become so busy making a living that we forget about making a life. Workplace politics and day-to-day deadlines take precedence over spending quality time with our work mates and loved ones, so we end up missing the forest because we're stuck in the trees.

Workplace Blues

What is it like at your workplace? Do you laugh a lot or is it strictly business? If your workplace is suffering from the blues, here are some ideas to perk it up. Yes, I know that some environments are more conservative than others, so have a look at these suggestions and adapt them to what would work for you.

- have a "fuzzy slippers, trashy jewelry and silly tie" day
- make a "fun ideas box" then ask people to contribute and use these ideas
- have a bubble-blowing contest
- create a smile packet and send it around. You'll have fun just making the packet
- have a "best of" contest, featuring funny one-liners from advertising slogans, for example, "a flush beats a full house"
- for warm fuzzies, keep stuffed toys in your office. Hide them in the drawer if you feel self-conscious and hug them frequently
- host a bring-your-child to work event. Watch how they discover and create magic

When we take charge of our schedules and create time to goof off in, we become healthier. When we choose to have more laughter in our lives, we stay that way. And every change begins with one little step.

Give Yourself a Mental Tune-Up

Let's tour our mental room. As important as physical exercise is, exercising the mind is also vital. It's a scientific fact that what we think affects our body, mind and spirit. We need to be thought-conscious. What do you say when you talk to yourself? Are you praising or condemning? An effective way of training the mind is to observe those negative thoughts and turn them around. Use the words *"cancel cancel"* to stop the downward spiral and quickly substitute a positive thought.

When I first became aware that I even had negative thoughts, I used a slogan. I said, *"thanks for sharing but we're doing things differently,"* whenever I caught an unhelpful thought and immediately substituted a helpful one. Initially I was vigilant about catching my thoughts, now I'm more relaxed. When I feel that darkness descending in me, as if my mind is sliding into a deep cesspool of slimy grime, I simply reach for the light, and grab onto a positive thought. It's simple and it works. For example, if I think I'm not going to get a speaking engagement, I silently say: "you always get the work you need" and that helps me stay in a positive frame of mind, whether the work materializes or not.

Be mindful of what you watch and read.

Substitute challenging reading and uplifting films for newspaper and television violence. Fill your mind with quality material because you love your mind and want to expand it.

Keep Agile

To keep my mind agile, I go on regular retreats, because I truly believe

"what you don't use, you lose."

Conferences are also something I attend to keep my edge and to grow in knowledge. And I read. Voraciously. All kinds of books: autobiographies, novels, business, psychology, self-help, spiritual odysseys and poetry—to flex my mental muscles.

For creative conditioning, I write in a journal for 10 minutes in the morning—writing down whatever comes out. I also sign up for some sort of exploration class (such as painting, acting, pottery or music) once a year with no expectation of being good at whatever I take. I focus instead on trying something new to activate my creative juices, expand my parameters and give me a new perspective.

Visit Your Spiritual Room

It's important to create room for spiritual replenishment in our lives. I've made a space in our bedroom that I call my sacred space. I've placed a little altar that has fresh flowers on it beside a favorite chair where I sit to meditate. Just seeing that chair helps me become serene. Beside my chair I have a shelf of spiritual books and uplifting music to bring me solace. Starting the morning with meditative practices gives me a heads up for the rest of the day.

Use Meditation

Meditation is helpful for quieting the mind and becoming focused. There is so much material available today about the benefits of meditation. Even if we only spend 10 minutes watching our thoughts and breathing, we will become more centered and less stressed. Affirmations, meditation, visualization, catching thoughts— they're all useful tools, the key is to pick up the tool that will bring you quality thinking.

Choose Inspirational Books

Choose uplifting reading to keep your mind primed. Find a daily meditation book to inspire you and read it regularly. Get another copy for your office or your car so you always have one with you. Subscribe to an inspirational newsletter on the Internet. Boost yourself up with spiritual support.

If you're working on a specific attribute, like patience, put "patience" on your computer screen saver. Write it boldly on a piece of paper and stick it on your refrigerator or near your bathroom mirror as a reminder.

Create a Gratitude List

According to research done by Michael McCullough, an associate professor of psychology at the University of Miami, gratitude makes us less susceptible to depression and kindles greater happiness in our lives. Developing an attitude of gratitude can be achieved by anyone.

I've learned to become grateful through listing five things I appreciate every evening before going to bed, starting with the fact that I've had another day to be grateful for. When I also begin my days this way, everything flows better. Gratitude is learned behavior, so right now I'm grateful that I have my daughter with me at the cottage and that we're working through our "stuff." I'm grateful that my cats are healthy, that the sun is shining, the refrigerator has good food in it and my computer is working. As I fill my mind with grateful pictures, I begin to see the bounty in my midst.

Keep an Open Heart

Brent, a fellow who restores log cabins, is a great model of spiritual contentment and openhearted acceptance. He is never too busy to reach out and offer a helping hand. "If you can't get out of your driveway, call Brent, he'll help anybody with anything," says Doug, a mutual friend. Brent emits a natural radiance; he wears a huge smile, he sees the best in everyone and people are naturally drawn to him.

When I give my love to others, when I lend a helping hand or a sympathetic ear, when I share a hug or a smile, I feel healthy and my immune system agrees.

Embrace Art

Each of the arts offers us mental, emotional and spiritual food. Music is very important in my life. The music in nature—rustling leaves, chirping birds, gurgling water, crashing waves. The music of the city—traffic, street noise, people. I listen to jazz, opera, folk, rock and classical music and what a feast there is to choose from! Mozart brings me to a higher consciousness, Bach makes my mind work, Joni Mitchell reminds me of my youth and Bob Seeger makes me dance. I spend time nurturing my esthetic senses by going to concerts, art galleries and theatre because my spirit yearns for the wonder of creativity and the celebration of beauty.

Intimacy

Once a week I visit my children and grandchildren to appreciate the treasures of love I have in my family. And I schedule time for quality lovemaking. Which means making sure that communication with my partner is in good shape, because without it nothing works. One of the advantages of becoming 50+ is that the hormones are not raging and the metabolism has slowed down, so I'm no longer at the mercy of lust. Doesn't mean I don't have it, I'm just not a slave to it.

These days, being vulnerable is a pre-requisite for being intimate. I like how Dr. William Masters defined good communication in a relationship: "It's the privilege of exchanging vulnerabilities." For me this means letting go of roles and expectations. Being able to really see the other and letting ourselves be seen. Telling the microscopic truth about what I'm feeling or experiencing in the moment and being able to hear the truth back without withdrawing or reacting. Touching, stroking, cuddling, laughing, sharing confidences, playing, exploring, giving and receiving are all aspects of making love and I need to plan time to make sure this sensuality gets expressed.

I also take time to connect with friends, time for gab-fests and get-togethers, for dinners and reflective talks. I try to create supportive and positive circles of intimacy and I make the effort to give back to my community.

Balance is challenging.

It sounds like there is a lot to do, but my activities are more about experiences to be lived than tasks to be done, plus I have a secret method of working them all in without getting stressed. Have you ever watched a tightrope walker balance on the high wire? It seems to me that they are poised in each moment, and they concentrate on taking one step at a time. Personally, I find balance challenging. Often I have so much going on that I don't take time to do the daily disciplines that keep me centered and fit, so here's what I do instead.

I cheat.

Remember that house with four rooms I spoke about at the beginning of this chapter? Well, instead of living in a 24-hour day, I live in 48-hour cycles. In 48 hours I can visit each one of my four rooms and practise a routine, which keeps me centered and productive.

Within 48-hours I can:

- take a half-hour walk or stretch my body through yoga
- eat vegetables, grains, fruit and protein and aim for seven hours of sleep
- clear my mind by sitting still for 10 minutes
- give myself soul time by listening to music, reading spiritual wisdom and helping others
- limber up mentally by reading a challenging article

Knowing I don't have to cram everything into just one day helps me create internal room and stay relaxed. According to the native myth, our inner house also has four doors. One door is for the past, one for the future, one for now and one for the present. We can spend some time opening the past door, but we don't want to get stuck there. We need to think about tomorrow, but not worry about it. We need to be aware of our "I want it now" compulsions, our tendency to grab at instant gratification, then let that go. The door that opens on the present is the door we need to keep open.

Be Here Now!

The last part of living healthy is about staying in the moment as much as possible. Knowing that each moment is precious and every moment is different. The more we can be here now the more alive we are. Being in this single moment; accepting whatever it brings us, breathing it in deeply and exhaling the waste of worry.

When we start worrying about tomorrow, we lose today. Being in the moment is difficult because we defend against it, perhaps because we can't control it. Paradoxically, when, through a moment of grace, we actually are totally present in the here and now, we see there is nothing to fear and we experience a deep peace. Whatever your now is, I urge you to accept it. Even the biggest sadness, the deepest fear, the strongest rage will evaporate if you truly embrace it.

The next time you feel pressured or squeezed by life, why be bound by the clock? Create your own time cycle. Visit each one of your four rooms regularly, enjoy whatever you're doing and remember: living healthy is accessible to anyone who makes the decision to do so.

Celebration Strategies

Tips for Healthy Living

1. Trust your intuition.
Listen to your inner voice. Try it out at the supermarket. Go food shopping after you've had a meal so that you're not hungry. Ask your body which foods it needs for nurturing, and then listen to what it has to say. Take yourself to a farmers' market and enjoy the lush colors and fresh selections. Buy food that will inspire and enliven you.

2. Commit to exercise you enjoy doing.
Choose something you enjoy doing and give this gift to yourself at least once a week. Make it official. Write down your choice below and your start-up date, then sign your name. This is your personal agreement, your contract with you. Honor it.

I _____, will start doing _____
on _____
signed _____ date _____

3. Play.

If you need to brighten your mood to get yourself started, find something red and fix your gaze on it for a while. This color has an energy-boosting effect, so when you want to get more playful, wear red!

4. Increase Serenity.

Give yourself plenty of down time. During the day, take frequent breath breaks, watch your thoughts, and read inspirational words. Turn your lips and thoughts upwards and smile.

Affirm Your Choices

When we feed ourselves good physical, mental, emotional and spiritual food, we are affirming our worth and making healthy choices.

The future is still under construction.

When we can view our lives as a process of awakening rather than a series of random events, it becomes easier to celebrate our entire being for all we have been, are now and will continue to be. Nothing that has happened in the past can be undone, so let it go. Concentrate on building a healthy lifestyle today by taking one little step at a time. Acknowledge your efforts, celebrate your success by giving yourself a pat on the back, and keep moving forward.

Affirmation. I take good care of my body, mind and spirit.
I enjoy healthy eating, exercising, laughing and relaxing.

Twelve

Embrace Death

I have listened to the realm of the spirit.
I have heard my own soul's voice, and
I have remembered that love is the
complete and unifying thread of existence.
Mary Casey

Throughout the whole of life one must
continue to learn how to live, and what will
amaze you even more, dear friends, one
must continue to learn how to die.
Seneca

I'm scared of dying. I admit it. A real chicken. Even writing these words down I notice my heart beats faster. I'm scared not so much of the dying itself as the stuff leading up to it. There is a part of me that would prefer to never mention the D word, unless it is D for Denial. My denial is designed to keep me comfortable but not to help me grow. So I want to talk openly about the mystery of death.

I wasn't around when my parents died. My father's last breath came in a hospital and I was on a holiday when my mother checked out of this physical world. I've missed the deaths of three close friends and my rationale has been that somehow I wasn't ready to handle death.

Well, I'm over 50 now and it's time I got acquainted with the death process, one of life's great adventures. I love adventure, and when I think of death that way, I can sidle up towards it.

Have you noticed that when you open up to learning something, the universe swiftly responds?

The call came on a Tuesday evening. Laura, Fraser's cousin, was dying. She'd been living in Indonesia for the past eight years and had returned to Canada with bone cancer. Although the first part of her life had been heavy with losses, during the latter part she had followed a path of personal happiness. She was 70. Three score years and ten.

Figuring she'd lived long enough, Laura made the decision to avoid treatment. She was an integral part of a spiritual community so she asked her closest friend, a member of the same community, if she could her die in her home. Hélène, her friend agreed. She and her husband had recently moved into a new house with a spectacular view, nestled in the midst of the Laurentian Mountains.

Other supporters rallied—a lifelong friend from Toronto, a retired nurse who lived nearby, and finally us: Fraser, her only cousin from Toronto, and me.

Laura had been given a month. The month had come and gone when we were called.

She hadn't wanted us to know, I suspect because once we were told it meant she really was dying. It is one thing to know you have a terminal illness and quite another to accept it I discovered.

Despite constant morphine injections and her shriveling body, Laura looked well. Her color was good, her mind alert. She'd fade off in the middle of a sentence, but when she'd come back, she'd know exactly what she had been saying and would finish her thought.

I learned to listen to the silences. Sitting at her bedside, sending her love, breathing in time with her breath, visualizing light around her face helped me transit from being afraid to being attendant.

Relieved of my self-imposed tyrannical to-do list and slavish obedience to daily routine, without familiar tasks to distract me or work to prepare, I learned to be more receptive to what was happening in the moment.

Death gave me time to "be" in.

Whether I was sponging Laura's tiny body, brushing her beautiful hair, or rubbing her dainty feet, I learned to become still in the pauses, neither finishing her thoughts, nor prompting her next words.

We were a strange little community. Together we embodied the four elements of the zodiac and many professions. Jean Pierre, a retired French lawyer and his therapist wife Hélène, were our hosts and Laura's chief caregivers. Then there was Herbert, a retired architect and her oldest friend, Beverley, an itinerant nurse, Fraser, a community college instructor, and me, a speaker/writer.

We shared bedside shifts and exchanged knowledge. We traded experiences; compressing lifetimes into anecdotes as we injected needles, administered sponge baths, changed diapers, shifted pillows.

After five days Laura was still with us. Waning, but with. Fraser returned to Toronto to prepare exams. I decided to stay with Laura. Being between engagements gave me time.

In my mind I thought I was giving. What was really happening was that I was receiving; getting important instruction on dying and therefore, living.

I think we die much as we live. My dad died drinking. My mother died quickly; that was her rhythm in life. While eating lunch she had a stroke, her head plopped down onto her plate and that was the end. Being with Laura, watching her choose a "conscious" death, propelled me to take a look at my living habits.

Most of my life I had equated living with doing—the more the better. Having adventures, accomplishing goals and compiling experiences. Now I saw that I'd been moving fast but not travelling far.

Living with Laura's imminent death meant being available and present in each moment. Staying alert with what was happening, relying on others and dropping my own agenda. It also meant living deliberately. Not saying those hurtful words when I felt thwarted or diminished—which generally occurred with Fraser. Living deliberately is a nice theory but hard to achieve. For instance, Fraser would be gently massaging Laura while I was balancing her energy, a skill I'd learned several years ago but hadn't practiced. Out of the corner of my eye I'd see Fraser move into my physical space, and I'd feel squeezed out, unimportant. Or I'd think he was working too long on one side of her body or going too deep with the massage. Non-verbally I'd try to get his attention and he'd ignore me, or worse, dismiss me with his hand. My anger would surface and I'd give him a look, sending mental daggers.

In retrospect I think we were going through the anger stage of the five stages of death so aptly identified by Elizabeth Kubhler-Ross. At the time, I knew I had to let go of wanting it to be "my way" and just let my reactions flow through me without acting on them. Like taking a mental shower, I concentrated on feeling my feelings then letting them wash through my body and drain out. That way I could be of use to Laura and still hold a space for the help Fraser was providing. He was her cousin after all! This is how I counselled myself, all the while being aware of my angry feelings.

Isn't it interesting how our primary relationships coax up the stuff within us we need to work on? I grabbed onto some ideas from *A Course in Miracles*.

I am determined to see this differently
You are never angry for the reason you think

My learning continued. I had to respect our communal space and remember to put things away immediately after using them. I learned to use containers for everything and live very simply. I could see how working a simple discipline created freedom. Living with order. Doing one thing at a time. Returning items to their place of origin. Back home, my apartment was full of clutter. I realized that I 'd been accumulating too much and dropping items on handy surfaces, then feeling swamped and overwhelmed

There was more, too. Staying aware of the common good, rather than just looking after my own needs or my husband's. Deferring. Being one of the group, not the leader or the star. Laura was the star. Her death was bridging the way to our being more conscious in living. She had gathered us all around her to help her leave. We each had a part to play, but she was in charge. Our job was to make her departure as smooth and painless as possible.

Six more days passed, each one offering me more to work on. I had to release my fear that she would just hang on for months, and I'd have to leave before she died. It was not on my clock or according to my plans that Laura would depart. This was between her and her creator.

I witnessed the stages her body went through, heard her labored breathing, saw her energy diminish and knew there was nothing I could do to stop the process. Yet a strange phenomenon was occurring. It seemed that the more her body withered, the clearer her inner light became. Her spirit radiated and her luminosity grew more evident as her body deteriorated. She was living her dying much as she'd lived her life—on her own terms, with courage and dignity. Seeking higher wisdom, sharing discoveries with love and generosity. Teaching us by example. What a gift! Whoever thinks that dying is awful hasn't had this uplifting experience. *Dying is a journey we each will take; yet we're not taught how to do it any more than we're taught how to live.*

One afternoon I was reading in her room when her breathing changed. Between the loud exhales there were fewer little inhales. A clawing, rasping sound came from her throat. Quickly I walked to her bed, then Beverley, the visiting nurse came in, followed by Hélène, Jean Pierre and Herbert.

"She's leaving us now," Beverly declared. "Romeo is coming to take her." (Romeo was Beverley's dear and departed husband.)

Jean Pierre started crying. We gathered around her bed and prayed. We must have been standing there for 10 minutes, listening to her struggle to breathe, convinced she was halfway to heaven, then suddenly Laura opened her eyes and her smile was joyous.

"Oh I feel so good, so loved, I love God and I love you all," she exclaimed, smiling sweetly at each one of us. Moments before she had been at death's door, her skin gray, her breathing labored, the whites of her eyes rolled upwards. Now she was fully present, laughing, playful and rapturous! As we stood around her bed she told us about the beautiful stars she'd been seeing and the fluffy clouds she'd gone through.

"And the light, did you see the light?" I queried

"No, no light, but it was all beautiful."

"My Romeo is here to take you," Beverly injected.

"Romeo, who is that?" Laura asked.

"He's my husband, you know I told you about him, I showed you his picture, remember?"

"How will I recognize him?" asked Laura.

"You won't have to find him, he'll find you. Close your eyes now and rest."

"But what about my children? Won't they be able to come and get me?" Laura had lost both her babies soon after they were born, lost them to cancer. Then her marriage fell apart and she started on her spiritual quest.

"Of course they can come and get you," I answered, sending Beverley the daggers now, wanting her to shut up, to let Laura be however she wanted to be, thinking how controlling and bossy nurse Beverly was, and knowing that the reason I was annoyed was because it was a reflection of me and my own bossiness. More lessons, all the time lessons.

I made the effort to love Beverley just as Laura did. Laura was truly loving and accepting of everyone, even in her dying. I need a lot of practice in this area. I love my family (until I get triggered by them), my seminar participants (because I call the shots) and my friends (because I need them), but often I walk around with judgments and withhold my affection. No more! I resolved to follow Laura's lead.

The doctor arrived. He'd been summoned to sign the death certificate, instead he saw a lively, beautiful woman beaming at everyone.

As Ken Tobias sang:

> *"Dying's a part of living,*
> *I'm sure you understand."*

Laura must have talked for about an hour before she drifted off into a peaceful soft sleep. The doctor said he'd never seen anything like her in his 40 years of practice, commenting on how clear she was despite weeks without food and strong doses of morphine.

"Perhaps it's because she's so spiritual," he offered, shrugging his shoulders.

"Perhaps it's because she doesn't want to leave," Hélène responded.

I thought they we're both right. Laura was receiving a lot of love, maybe more than she'd ever had, and that would be hard to let go of.

Two weeks later, best friend Herbert packed up, Hélène and Jean Pierre were drained, I felt spent, and Laura was still with us, bolting upright during the nights, trying to get out of bed. She'd had no food and hardly any water for a month. What was she living on? Hélène spent every night with her; we were all exhausted, yet Laura endured. Was it her will? Was she afraid, even though she professed not to be? Was she staying to help us learn something more?

One morning she turned to me with despair in her eyes. "We made a covenant that we would spread love, that we would be true, but we have broken that promise. We must not break our promise. I will die screaming that we mustn't break our promise, God please help us all," she pleaded.

I tried to tell her we humans are slowly improving, that each day more and more people are learning that love is what we are here to give, but she was dismayed by what she saw. She was making her way to wherever she was going and as she was leaving she could see what we were doing on our planet; and her heart was breaking.

My own heart ached as I watched life ebb out of her.

We were interchangeable now, the I that is we. Part of me was leaving with Laura and my own life force felt diminished, yet at the same time part of her was moving into me.

Fraser returned, bringing city angst and a shield around his heart. He found fault with all of us and sought refuge in his book. Even though I knew he was hiding because he was in pain, I felt hurt that he didn't give her more, or support me better. Laura was becoming my mother whose death I missed, my friend who died alone in Mexico. As Laura died, other deaths converged in me and I was now present for all of them.

My body held the emotional toll. My shoulders felt stabbed by a hundred sharp knives. I hadn't had a bowel movement in a week, I felt bloated and overextended. With Laura I could be loving and giving, yet even hearing her desperate exhortation that "we mustn't break our promise to love one another" and promising to give that love, I found myself feeling helpless and angry then yelling at Fraser, projecting my pain on him, stuck in the trap of reacting.

"Do not go gentle into that good night . . . Rage, rage against the dying of the light," Dylan Thomas' words reverberated. Then, like a quick thunderstorm, my ranting passed and the angry energy abated, giving me relief. There was movement in my body again. My shoulders softened, the letting go had begun.

"First the opening, then the retreat, then the letting go." I remembered these words from some long-forgotten movie. They struck a chord then, now I understood them.

"The Lord is my shepherd, I shall not want." Over and over again Laura and I repeated these few words together. It says it all. If we believe there is a Lord of love who takes care of us, there is nothing wanting.

Sitting beside her bed, watching the thoughts my mind spun, I longed for a blank mind, a meditative peace. Why was it so hard to achieve? I sat and thought about writing or doing my yoga. I thought about all the pounds I had gained because I was eating so much. I thought and I judged. Even while emptying my mind, it filled up with more trivia.

I asked myself, "So what's the lesson? To accept that this is how it is?" I watched Laura breathe, heard her sweet exclamations— and never a complaint—felt her kisses on my hand, noticed the small things. Is that what life was all about? Would I ever learn to let go? Would she?

Laura was moving rapidly towards her destination, but aren't we all? I might be next. Will I be anywhere near as gracious as she was? Perhaps the lesson is to live each moment gracefully, with some of the courage I gained from being with Laura.

Life is a crapshoot. None of us know in advance when it is our turn to roll the dice.

Each one of us knows people who are presently dying or have passed on. No one gets out of here alive, yet many of us live in denial, pretending to ourselves that we have endless amounts of time left or that we're so strong and powerful somehow we'll defy the gods or nature or history. As long as we don't really have to think about our death, we can just carry on . . . as if.

Then that moment comes—our moment—when we're called to let go of our lives. And the question arises: have we truly lived each precious moment? When it's too late, do we think of what might have been? Are we ready for the final review of our lives, ready to look at how we neglected or hurt people, including ourselves?

I guess those everyday losses we experience throughout our time on earth help us prepare for our final leave-taking. Over the course of our lives we die many little deaths. With each sickness or loss we get a chance to know our fallibility and let go of our attachments. Each time we fall short of our goal or admit mistakes and failures, our ego—our arrogance—dies a little. All of which prepares us for our final letting go.

Native North Americans have a saying: "Today is a good day for dying." When I first heard this, I was shocked. Then I thought about it and concluded if we incorporate death into our lives, if we keep the notion of it close, like a cozy warm sweater, then both our living and our dying will be more celebratory, so yes, today's a good day for dying.

From a friend who has AIDS: "You've just got to live each day the best you can. That's it, that's all there is!" This is what Laura was doing, what most of us are doing, come to think of it.

One day after lunch, I was sitting upstairs, going through my mail, then trying on the fur jacket Laura had bequeathed me, pirouetting in it to show Fraser. Hélène and Jean Pierre were out. Fraser and I had been sitting with Laura the day before, staying until late into the night. She'd slipped into a coma, and now neither one of us could make our legs walk down the stairs to be by her bedside.

I kept procrastinating, avoiding, until finally I ran out of excuses and announced I was going downstairs.

As soon as I entered the room I knew. There is a stillness to death, an unmistakable emptiness. I felt it right away and felt the fear as well. Standing on that final step, holding my breath and looking at her, I bolted upstairs for Fraser. "Come down sweetheart, I think Laura has gone." Quickly he ran down the stairs and we both went to her side.

Her face was still warm, although it was clear that her body was a mere shell. At the corner of her left eye a crystal tear lingered. There was a sense of peace now, no more struggle.

"Do we have to die to find this peace?" I wondered.

I felt shame as I realized that Laura must have died while I was prancing about in her coat! As I began to self-flagellate I remembered what a good friend once told me, that often people prefer to leave when no one is around.

It makes sense. It would be hard to go with loved ones holding your hand, binding the earthly ties. Before her coma I'd spent many hours loving Laura, and I knew she felt it. Still the nagging thought remains that I'd copped out. I have to live with the knowledge that my fear prevailed at the last minute. Next time I'll do better. I'm a work in progress after all. I suspect I'll have more opportunities to practise helping others in their leave-taking before I go myself. I won't run from these invitations. Being with Laura during this precious time gave me a deeper appreciation for life.

I am grateful for the rain today, for the scent of the flowers, the music on the radio. Most especially for the loved ones in my life.

I have changed. I feel softer and lighter in my own body and at the same time more grounded. Laura's dying was a call to me to accept my finite being, and make adjustments in my life. There is only so much time ahead and I must choose how I live my moments, not just do it by rote. Energy is precious and I need to care for mine.

These days I ask myself: *"Self, is this the best choice for me?"* When I am asked to do something or when I turn to the fridge for comfort, I remind myself I have a choice. Change doesn't last without reinforcement, so today I'm going to call that nearby neighbor who lives alone and suggest we go for a walk.

I am grateful for the depth that Laura helped me reach, and for the love I was able to share with her. The dreaded boogeyman has disappeared; I discovered death had no sting, no final dominion, for in my mind's eye I can see Laura dancing jubilantly in the light.

Postscript

Two months later, Fraser and I returned to visit Laura's gravesite, which Hélène had selected and lovingly tended. Holding hands, we could hear Laura's silvery laughter, sense her joy. We could see her dancing.

Hélène is painting again, and seems to have abundant energy. Herbert is studying *A Course in Miracles*, Beverley has found someone else to love and Fraser and I are not arguing much anymore. I have given away bags of clothing and reduced some of my clutter. Thanks to Laura, I now have a relationship with one of her very special friends, who has become my spiritual mentor. Little miracles have happened!

Celebration Strategies

Embrace your dying

1. Talk about it.

Even though we intellectually understand that dying is part of living and that everything comes full circle and no-one is exempt, it is still difficult for many of us to address this disquieting and often shunned subject. A good start would be to break the silence and open up to the inevitable fact of dying. We could invite our friends to explore thoughts and feelings about death and dying.

2. Self-probe.

You could start to self probe by asking these questions:
What do I believe will happen when my life is over?
Where do I get my beliefs from?
Do these beliefs serve me?
Once you have tenderly approached the subject of your own death, you might want to share any uneasiness you have with a trusted friend or spiritual advisor.

3. Do your research.

There are many books you can read on the subject and little things you can do. Check out the local library for books on aging and death or try volunteering at a senior's residence or long-term care facility. Helping people at the end of their lives can be fulfilling and insightful. As I discovered, what you receive in those environments can far surpass what you give.

If you are given the opportunity to be with a friend or loved one as they approach death, please take full advantage of the privilege. You will emerge with precious gifts. One of the blessings I've received is that by facing our dying we become more committed to living, and by going through the fear of death we emerge with great respect for life.

Affirmation: Today is a good day for dying!

Thirteen

Design Your Life

*You must decide if you want to act or react,
deal your own cards or play with a stacked
deck. And if you don't decide which way to
play with life, it always plays with you.*
Merle Shain

*There is a guidance for each of us, and by
lowly listening we shall hear the right word
... Place yourself in the middle of the stream
of power and wisdom which flows into your
life. Then, without effort, you are impelled
to truth and to perfect contentment.*
Ralph Waldo Emerson

*"It does not matter how slowly you
go so long as you do not stop."*
Confucius

What constitutes a great life? Clearly, having a picture of what you want—and don't want—is an important start.

Here's a simple test. If you wake up with a feeling of anticipation instead of dread, it's a good sign. If you get out of bed stressed because you're already running behind schedule, the odds are against your having a Celebration day.

How easy it is to waste our lives, doing what we think we should do. Letting other people's standards rule us, instead of figuring out our own. Too late Shakespeare's Richard II laments, "I have wasted my life, now my life wastes me." That mournful refrain is one we want to avoid. And yet, "Most people die with their music still in them," said Oliver Wendall Holmes.

It's important to hear our music and equally important to play it. Are you playing your music? Singing your heart's song?

For many years I went along with what other people wanted, not even aware that I had a choice. I thought I had to accommodate their needs. I believed I was responsible for their happiness.

I spent half of my life trying to please others before I woke up.

Today, because I have learned to trust my inner voice, I can genuinely respond to other people with kindness and empathy. I know I'm responsible for my attitude and choices, and my number one job is to take care of me. This is very liberating. It also means I can't blame another person for my foul plays.

When I decided to leave teaching and start my own business it was a big risk. I had a teenage son at home and about $250 dollars in the bank. No prospects, no contacts and no retirement fund. I gave up the security of a regular income because of a desire to fulfill an inner longing.

I wanted to help others break through negative beliefs and shift anger patterns. I was burning with passion to share what I had learned and that passion gave me the courage to strike out on my own.

Several years later I saw my friends taking early retirement with healthy pensions and I felt envious, wondering if I'd made the right decision.

One day, out of the blue, I had a phone call from a high school principal that went like this: "Angela, I have your name down on my list as having taught successfully for 11 years. As you may know, we're experiencing a shortage of qualified teachers right now and I'm wondering if you'd be interested in returning to teaching?"

I was tempted. My work is erratic, my retirement savings nominal. I live what some people would call an unbalanced and anxiety-producing life. Sometimes I'm in the fast lane, cramming all my effort into a few weeks or months. Other times there are big white spaces in my calendar.

No work = no money. I struggle to juggle through the lean times.

And then there's my work environment. My desk, situated in the living room of our apartment, is littered with mail, bills, to-do lists and scraps of paper. Filing gets done at night or on weekends. Being in my own business means working late into the night, thinking, planning, preparing, designing—all unpaid.

When preparing for a presentation, I ruminate about how to make the most impact, wondering what will help people, how I can offer them the best in me and fulfil their objectives. I'm constantly honing my craft, trying out new ideas, thinking of how I can ignite interest and sow seeds of hope. Then there's the presentation itself: gearing up with nervous anticipation, experiencing exhilaration while I'm on stage and suffering the post-presentation blues. These are all part of the package. It seems I'm always auditioning for the job. Plus, it's a lonely business. There are no team members rooting in the wings, only me, second-guessing myself.

Having said that, I want you to know that

I feel privileged to be doing what I love to do.

I get paid to speak to people about ideas I believe in and share solutions I've found useful. I watch eyes light up and see heads nod when people hear something they consider valuable. I meet wonderful folks who tell me how my information has changed their lives. This is very rewarding. Plus there are job perks, like traveling to interesting places and staying in fine hotels.

What tempted me in the principal's teaching offer was the regular salary and the pension.

I realized my motive was wrong. I was thinking about the money, not the kids. In truth, I no longer wanted to teach in a high school. So I thanked her and said no.

Going through that exercise reminded me that there are always career decisions to ponder and life choices to make. Consequences to each action and no guarantees.

I enjoy my roller-coaster life with its ups and downs, which means it is pointless to complain about lacking job security. In hindsight I can see how I have been guided to create the life I love to live. My early experience of having a dad who told me stories sparked my own storytelling and gave me tools of the trade I might never have developed. And those years I spent in foster homes taught me how to navigate unknown territory and overcome the fear of rejection. This training has been vital for both my speaking and writing profession.

Which leads to the questions:

- **What has been vital for you to learn?**
- **How are you framing your life experience?**
- **Are you already living the life you love to live? If so, congratulate yourself. If not, what does your ideal life look like?**

Start by seeing the picture of your idyllic work life in your mind. Here's how. Get comfortable, sit quietly, close your eyes and take a few deep breaths. Now begin to imagine your ideal work situation. Notice what is going on around you. Are you in a building? Outdoors? Alone? With others? If there are people around, observe them. What are they doing and saying? Can you see their facial expressions? The colors they are wearing? How do they move? Come back to yourself now. See yourself doing what you love to do and notice how you feel. See the expression on your face. Take it all in. Enlarge the picture, as if you are blowing up a giant photograph. Anchor the photo by touching a part of your body with your right hand. As you imprint the image of yourself doing what you love to do, you will strengthen your resolve to actually create it.

Gently open your eyes and write out what you saw. Take all the time you need. Whenever you wish to recall this powerful picture, simply relax and touch the "anchor" part of your body with your right hand and enjoy the replay.

Now ask yourself these two questions:

- Do I have the courage to go for the work I love?
- Will I choose to risk to lose so that I can win?

Risk: There is always a risk when we choose to sing our heart's song. Who knows the outcome in advance?

Lose: You might have to let go of doing what you're doing now. That's the rub. Your work may not be supportive of who you are and you may have to forgo security.

Win: Either way it's a win because of the growth. There will be growth and change, the zing of adventure. Because of your willingness to change, you will develop faith. The courage to step out of the familiar and into the unknown is what faith is all about. It's by little acts of faith that we reap some of our greatest rewards.

Become a Willing Life Participant

The highest reward for the work we do is not what we get for it, it is what we become by doing it. Self respect and satisfaction become daily doses of feeling good about ourselves. Which means doing what we are meant to be doing, taking risks and becoming willing participants in life. Make the decision to follow your passion and see where it leads you.

Next have a look at your relationships. Again, ask yourself: Do I have the courage to create a loving relationship? Will I choose to risk to lose so that I can win? If you are not in a relationship now you might want to create a vision board. Buy a sheet of Bristol board, gather some magazines and glue, put on some music and enjoy discovering. Start to explore your magazines, cutting out images and words that attract you.

When you are finished selecting and cutting, paste your images and words onto the Bristol board. Step back and survey your creation. Notice what is forefront. What is your picture telling you? Commit to looking at your vision board every day. Allow your vision to work its magic upon you. Before long you will see the symbols on your board beginning to appear in real-life situations.

When I wanted to be in a love relationship again, I wrote out a list of 10 qualities I wanted in a mate, then I made another list of 10 qualities I had to offer. I put both of these lists in a book and promptly forgot about them. Two weeks later, Fraser showed up. Later I reviewed my list and found that he was everything I'd written down. Once we were in relationship, I made a vision board of commitment, and two years later we were married. It worked out beautifully, right down to the honeymoon cruise I'd pasted on my board. Seeing is believing and believing is seeing!

> *"Come to the edge"*
> *"No we cannot, we are afraid."*
> *"Come to the edge."*
> *"No we cannot, we'll fall."*
> *"Come to the edge."*
> **And they came, and he pushed them, and they flew!**
> Apollinaire

What risk will you take? When will you make the changes you need to make? Remember the personal assessment you did in Chapter One? Are you willing to create the life you love to live?

The main thing is to keep the main thing the main thing. If you want more love, give love. If you want more joy, be joyous. Look for the good in all things and stay open to receiving life's gifts.

Set Realistic Goals

If you like to work with goals, start setting both long and short-term goals. Spend a few minutes each day writing out your daily goals, then glance over your long-range plans. The reason for doing this is to stay on track. Sometimes we get so bogged down with daily details that we forget about our dreams. We think we're working to pay down debts instead of living to express our deepest purpose. Make a plan. Carve out your turf. Set your sights, dream your dreams and go for those moments that take your breath away.

> **Hold fast to dreams**
> **For if dreams die**
> **Life is a broken-winged bird**
> **That cannot fly.**
> **Hold fast to dreams**
> **For when dreams go**
> **Life is a barren field**
> **Frozen with snow.**
> Langston Hughes

For example, if you want to write or paint but the self-talk says:

- *"I have young children and a spouse to consider"*
- *"I'm a single parent and the sole support of these young children"*
- *"I'm already exhausted, and there's no way I can re-design my life and follow my dream"*
- *"I have to work every day"*

. . . make friends with your critical voice, then build a plan. Start by using one or two lunch hours a week. Buy a notebook, or a sketch-pad, get away from your workplace, go outside if you can, or to a café and begin. Write down your thoughts; start sketching what is in front of you. Take another two hours on the weekends. Which might mean you have to get up earlier or hire a sitter or make an exchange arrangement with a friend. By doing this you'll have created 16 hours a month! When you have something written or painted, show it to people, get some feedback and take the next step.

I hear my mother's voice saying: "Where there's a will there's a way." There are ways! We just have to stay open to possibilities. First you need to know what you want. If you change your plan later, no problem. If you don't have a plan to change, and catch yourself feeling like a victim, change your mind. Get focused, stay present and live a day at a time.

Live with Joy

> *Look to this day,*
> *For it is life,*
> *The very life of life.*
> *For yesterday is but a dream,*
> *And tomorrow is only a vision,*
> *But today, well lived,*

Makes every yesterday a dream of happiness
And every tomorrow a vision of hope.
Look well, therefore, to this day.
Sanskrit proverb

There's a knowing within each one of us that understands how to live life fully and hold time lightly. How to enjoy a sunset or a snowfall just because it's happening. How to open our arms to others without expectation. And there's also a knowing about what we need in our lives and how to fulfill these needs. Yes, pain is necessary, but

suffering is optional and joy is a choice.

I think we need joy as much as we need food and clothing, sometimes even more. A joyful moment for me can be chopping vegetables to make a hearty winter's soup, gasping with delight when I see summer fireflies glowing and darting as twilight turns into night, swishing my feet through the brilliance of falling autumn leaves. Beauty is all around us, all we have to do is keep our eyes open and celebrate what we see.

Each of us has days in our lives that are marked by big celebrations, but what about the little ecstasies that keep our daily activities from becoming dreary drudgery? Can you build in petite celebrations? Can you savor mini-moments? Will you map out time for discoveries and adventures? Too many people go through life dutifully serving some imagined master, never realizing their life belongs to them. I don't want you to travel this route. Oh no, you need a life that is reflective of who you are, one that expresses how you want to live. We're not talking perfection here, but we are talking design and commitment.

If you don't design your life, who will?

If not now . . . when?

Here are some Celebration Strategies to keep you focused.

Celebration Strategies

Design your Life of Celebration

1. Write out what you wish to change.

2. Create your own company.
Not your own business, *your own company*. Call it Me Inc!
Write out time for Me Inc. on every page of your planner for the
next month. Then ask: *"How can I nurture me?"* Write your
preferences in your calendar. I'm big on the three m's—movies,
massage and moments of madness.

3. Take a backward glance over your life.
List your significant times or events—the traumas and
triumphs. Then survey your list. How did you handle failures?
Sorrows? Joys? Do you notice any themes? For example, is
your life a life of struggle? If so, what does this say about your
belief systems? Is there any room for adjustment here?

4. Go back to your Personal Self-Assessment in Chapter One.
What areas did you discover that needed help? Do you want to
be more balanced? Healthy in mind and body? Are you taking
time to play? Do you need more quiet time alone in nature or
communing with your higher power? Can you listen to others
without wanting to finish their sentences? Do you challenge
your mind? Are you ready to have it all? Look over your answers
again, look deeply.

When you can clearly see what you've created thus far, you will have a much better idea of what you want the next section of your life to be like, and you can design it with flair and fervor.

5. Ask yourself what resources you have to make your dreams come true.

What's your "first things first?" Where will you begin? By the way, you don't have to solve every problem to achieve your dream life, you just have to have the intention and start moving in the right direction.

Affirmation: I am willing to design the life I love to live.

Fourteen

Celebrate!

For this is wisdom: to live,
To take what fate, or the Gods, may give.
Laurence Hope

"What has helped you over the great obstacles
of life?" was asked of a very successful
man. "The other obstacles," he answered.
Napoleon Hill

Dance with life as your partner! Although
some days you may feel like you have two
lead feet, you can still keep in step.
Kim Good

Turning 50 was a major event in my life. I wanted my mother, who was living in a nursing home at the time, to commemorate the occasion by taking me to dinner. In fact, I wanted her to take the whole family, and after some convincing and cajoling, she agreed. Decreeing that I was entering the "fabulous 50s," I threw away my tatty underwear and bought scarlet red replacements, which I wore under an elegant pinstriped black pantsuit that accentuated my spiky short haircut. Burgeoning with excitement, I made reservations at one of my favorite restaurants.

My daughters and their mates, my grandchildren and my partner were in attendance. We ate, we drank, and finally the bill came. The waiter took my mother's credit card and in a few moments he returned and whispered something to my mother. "What was that? Speak up young man," my mother declared. "I'm sorry, but your credit card doesn't work," the waiter repeated, shrugging his shoulders with a tinge of embarrassment.

"Then fix it," she snapped back, dismissing him with a flourish of her wrist. The upshot was that I had to pay the entire tab! Later I thought about how appropriate it was. My arrogance and delusions of grandeur had cost me a few hundred dollars and had given me some food for thought, which foreshadowed the fabulous 50s.

The 50s have been fabulous. I've learned to celebrate life as if it's a "come as you are" party, and it is okay for me to be who and how I am. I've put some of my ghosts to rest, and forgiven those who have hurt me. I've learned to give myself more time. Gradually I'm letting go of the "should be" judgments and savoring the reality of what life has to offer, moment by moment.

Funny isn't it that those standout moments are often so different from what we imagine. It's not the special events, the dress-up clothes, the trophies or the champagne toasts that I hold dear—although those have all been wonderful. It's the comfort of spending time with old friends and laughing about how we used to be. It's being with family, sharing the ups and downs of our lives. It's listening to the rain and being grateful the roof doesn't leak.

Today I lunched with Nancy, a good friend and successful artist. Her studio houses an explosion of colour, a plethora of equipment. Bright fabric for making people-dolls and purses are stacked on counters beside multicoloured wool skeins ready for weaving. Thousands of delicate beads lie next to chartreuse, lemon and raspberry felt strips, which will be used for wall hangings. Exquisite glazes surround great vats of clay; bright acrylic paints vie for her canvas. It's all there, ready and available.

Nancy works in one medium for a while and when she gets stuck, she reaches for another. What a grand life metaphor this is. When we feel ourselves getting stuck, we can simply look around us, pick up something else, move to a different medium and gain a fresh perspective.

It's so easy to get caught in a rut, spinning our wheels and taking life for granted. Easy to forget to be grateful for small joys, like the knowing smile of a loved one, or the sedating purr of a contented cat. How, five minutes after he starts reading, the glasses slide down my partner's nose as his head droops and the sputtering snores begin. How the sunlight catches the red-golden glint of my daughter's curls. How I always get to be Ken to my granddaughter's Barbie, and even though she pretends to be embarrassed about the song I made up for her, she has it memorized. These are the moments that make my life so rich. My young granddaughter is quite convinced if I change a word in the songs I sing to her, then I must be doing it wrong. She doesn't know yet that change will be her constant companion in life, her next opportunity knocking.

What I've discovered is that the difficulties we face, the challenges we overcome are life's biggest treasures. It's like the way pearls and diamonds are formed: from grit in the shell and from the pressure of the earth. By going through those hard times we uncover precious inner gems like compassion and resourcefulness, which we can use to make our lives and our world a better place.

When I think the world is an unfair place to live in, then my world looks like an unfair place to live in. When I cling to the notion that life should be like a picture I make up, I continue to suffer disillusionment and disappointment. The cause of suffering for most people is the dissatisfaction they project on the world they live in.

**Become an active agent in your
perception of the world.**

When my granddaughter Meiping was asked what she wanted for Christmas last year, the only thing she had on her list was to sponsor a foster child in the Third World. Taking small steps towards looking outside yourself to the bigger world can also change how you view your personal life and immediate surroundings.

It takes courage to change and to face life on life's terms.

It means we have to adjust our thinking, and realize that we are in charge of how we see our world and all the people in it.

We can choose to alter our perspective. Today I live in "I don't know." Not having to have answers, enjoying the questions, being content with what comes my way. Open to receiving what my Higher Power has in store for me.

Every night before I go to bed I review my day. If it hasn't been a cause for celebration, I let go of the "should have, would have, could have's" then find something to be grateful for.

The biggest key to celebrating life is to develop practical gratitude. Become willing to put in the effort.

Look for the small things, the everyday miracles.

Start by waking up in the morning thankful for the freshness of a new day. Enjoy stretching your body. Take a moment to gaze at the sky. Breathe deeply. Savor the ping of splattering raindrops. Notice the lush greenness of summer and watch as leaves turn golden, then russet in autumn. Find the sculpted bluish white shapes, which almost seem to breathe, on a moonlit winter's night. Watch mist hover above water. Make time to notice and delight in the panorama of life. Pay attention to what is in front of your eyes, the profusion of colors, the parade of seasons, the exquisite beauty of it all!

Learn from your errors, and forgive others theirs. This is how you train yourself in practical gratitude. With daily appreciations.

When we're grateful for whatever comes our way, no matter how small or how difficult, we are truly living a life of celebration. When we see our universe as abundant, when we seek out ways to make a contribution, we find insights and opportunities beckoning.

Some days are sparkly diamonds, while other days are heavy stones, but each day is precious. I am particularly blessed this year, because I have a new grandbaby, Tovan Alexander, who, as I write this, is 10 months old. What delight this beautiful child brings! How irresistible he is. All I want to do is look at him in amazement and kiss him and hug him, as if in so doing I could mould him to me and keep him close forever. There is nothing like new life to remind us how precious life is, and how we can never take it for granted. Although I love to watch Tovan learn to crawl and now stand, a part of me wants to freeze him and keep him small forever, keep him as a happy round Buddha baby, full of joy and smiles, untouched by life's vicissitudes. Ah, but that would be denying him life's experiences, wouldn't it? I have to reach out for acceptance and shine some light on my wishful thinking. Once again, acceptance takes me home.

Please don't waste your energy bemoaning your fate, your past and your circumstances. Seize this moment and do something with it. Create a life beyond your wildest dreams. Go for your own gusto. Connect with others. You are so beautiful! If you could only see yourself as you really are: a magnificent unique creation. There is nobody else quite like you. That alone is a reason to celebrate. Even if you don't believe in yourself this minute, you will learn to.

Deborah Szekely was in her 70s when she founded Eureka Communities, a grassroots effort to train leaders of the most dynamic inner city non-profit organizations to mentor and share success stories. Every year Deborah climbs Mt. Kuchucomes—five miles of climbing—and she goes straight to the top.

"What keeps you so alive?" she was asked.

"I'm so curious about what's going to happen next. I always think there's more ahead than there was behind," she replied.

"There are two things to aim at in life: first,
to get what you want and, after that, to enjoy it.
Only the wisest of mankind achieve the second."
Logan Pearsall Smith

The people you meet, the new things you learn, the experiences you compile, the choices you make, the days and moments of your life—all are seeds with limitless potential to bear fruit. You can't always control the seeds that fall into your life, but you can control the way they're planted and cared for. Each moment has a lifetime of possibilities. Think of that! You can change the course of the rest of your life right now, this very instant, if you want to.

Choose to celebrate yourself. Choose to celebrate others, for

The love in your heart wasn't put there to stay,
Love isn't love, 'till you give it away!
Anon

Use my Celebration Strategies. They work!

Celebration Strategies

1. Develop a clear and agile mind.

Practice meditation to focus and still that incessant head chatter. Make a ritual of giving yourself time every day to be still. Aim for little pauses at the end of sentences, and notice how the pauses grow. Rid your mind of negative thought patterns. Embrace new concepts. Keep learning. Learn about the computer, gardening, crafts, cooking. Learn about others.

2. Create a belief system that supports you.

Release any blame or victim beliefs that keep you in bondage. Know that the same wild wind blows on us all—and it's not the wind, it's the set of our sails that determines how far we go.

It's not what happens to us, it's how we interpret what happens to us, and how we handle it, that grows our character. Develop beliefs that work for you.

3. Trust your intuition.

Pay attention to those inner nudges. Follow your hunches. Honor who you are. Trust that you have the golden key and use it to unlock your intuitive door. One way to confirm your intuition is to ask: "Is this for my higher good?" If it is, act on it.

4. Know that every being on earth has a talent and a purpose.

There are no mistakes. Be still long enough to discover what your purpose is and embrace it with enthusiasm.

5. Learn from everything.

Use P.E. 101 (Personal Experience, heavy dues). Observe what you have learned from your challenges and successes. Notice what worked and what did not. Find the gift in each situation. Profit from O.P. (Other People). Learn from their experiences. What a wonderful way to learn. Almost like going to the fairgrounds and not having to pay the admission price. Learn from other people's challenges. Hear what they did that didn't work; pay attention to what they changed as a result.

Learn from what you see around you. Like ants: watch how they all work together in unison, dragging away that little piece of food. Notice the tree leaves. Think about how they simply endure, day after day, through heat and wind and rain and until one day they turn different colors and slowly fall away, leaving space for new leaves.

Make space for new ideas to grow. Keep your eyes, your ears and most importantly, your heart tuned up and open. Be a lifetime learner.

6. Develop a winning attitude.

Correct old errors in judgment. Release resentments and do your forgiveness work so you can be whole. Remember that others are learners just like you. Some are slow learners. Sometimes we need to forgive and sometimes we need to put up "No Trespassing" signs. Sometimes we just need to hang in. Make time to be with cheerful friends who boost your self-esteem. Surround yourself with what you love, be it family, pets, keepsakes, music, plants or books.

7. Build daily spiritual disciplines.

Practice yoga, tai chi, chanting or meditation. Pray. Let your home environment reflect your essence. Consider what Abe

Lincoln said. "I don't know much about religion, all I know is that when I do good, I feel good."

8. Keep your creative juices flowing.

Write in a journal, take a painting class, draw with your non-dominant hand, dance, sing or fly a kite. Build shelves, paint stones, string beads, knit. Go deep-sea diving. Watch cheerful movies. Do whatever you love to do as often as possible. Be alive while you are living!

9. Do the best you can.

Do what you can as best as you can. Value your health. If it is good, preserve it. If it is shaky, improve it. Let yourself enjoy what you accomplish. Give yourself plenty of acknowledgment. Stop trying to be perfect, it's waste of time. We're not supposed to be perfect, we're supposed to be human. Be a good human.

10. Stay open to miracles.

If you believe in them, they will happen. Miracles have been reserved for each one of us. Every day miraculous events occur. Watch for them.

11. Live in the now.

Embrace each moment fully. Especially the hard ones. Show up. Breathe. Let the tears happen. Endure, grieve and move on. Relish the simple things.

12. Celebrate!

Love and play and learn a little every day. Overlook lots. Give generously. Tell the people you love that you love them, at every opportunity. Laugh until you gasp for breath. Smile at strangers. Stay grateful.

Remember, as George Carlin says, "Life is not measured by the number of breaths we take, but by the moments that take our breath away." Give yourself those breathtaking moments. No matter how old you are, or how young, there is time today for you to express your uniqueness and behold the brilliance of others.

My friend Jane Hewitt had a lifelong fear of heights so on her 82nd birthday she decided to go skydiving.

"What was it like Jane?" I asked her.

"Bloody terrifying but exhilarating. I'm glad I did it and I don't have to do it again," she answered.

Before her skydive Jane had not traveled for many years. Next year she plans to visit Turkey. And that's the way it works. One step leads to the next step, which leads to the next step and pretty soon you're so far along in your celebration journey that you can't even remember a time when you weren't.

We are pilgrims on a journey,
Fellow travelers on the road
We are here to help each other
Walk the distance, bear the load.

I will hold the light for you
In the night-time of your fear:
I will reach my hand out to you,
Speak the peace you long to hear.

I'll be there when you are hurting
When you laugh I'll laugh with you;
I will share your joys and sorrows
Till we've seen this journey through.

Put your best foot forward, start walking and celebrate!

I'll be with you in spirit.

---

1 The Servant Song, written by Richard Gillard © 1977 *Scripture In Song*, adapted here
  by Angela Jackson.

Bibliography, References and Recommended Reading

The following are references to publication's I've mentioned throughout the book, and books I've found useful along my journey.

A Course In Miracles, Foundation for Inner Peace, Penguin Books, New York, 1977, 1996.

A Return To Love, Williamson, Marianne, HarperCollins, New York, 1993.

The Ecstatic Journey, Burnham, Sophy. Ballantine Publishing Group, New York, 1997.

Love Yourself Thin, Moran, Victoria. Daybreak Books, New York, 1997.

New Passages, Mapping your Life across Time, Sheehy, Gail. G Merritt Corp, Random House of Canada Ltd., Toronto, 1995.

Wherever You Go There You Are, Kabat-Zinn, Jon, Hyperion, New York, 1994.

Who Will Cry When You Die? Sharma, Robin S. HarperCollins, Toronto, 1999.

About the Author

ANGELA JACKSON is an internationally respected authority on anger management and life balance. Her first book, *Celebrating Anger* is a Canadian bestseller and has been published in German and Chinese.

Angela's power as a speaker and writer comes from her personal experience. She is a graduate of the University of Toronto, York University and the School of Hard Knocks. She has been featured on CBS *Geraldo*, CBC *Venture*, *Body Break*, *Benmurgi Live*, *Real Life* TV and has contributed to leading publications.

Angela's background in education, counseling and business and her commitment to help people relate in a positive fashion, has made her one of Canada's most sought after presenters. The mother of three grown children, she resides in Toronto, Muskoka and Florida with her husband and two cats.

To learn more about Angela Jackson's keynotes and seminars, visit: **www.angelajackson.com** or email **angel.speak@sympatico.ca**.

Keynotes, Seminars and Personal Coaching with **Angela Jackson,**

Best-selling Author and Professional Speaker

In a presentation style that has been described as energizing and engaging, Angela motivates people to take responsibility for their lives and actions. Known as "the Speaker with Heart " her talent is to help people master the necessary skills to deal with challenging emotions and stress. Whether it's an exciting, thought provoking keynote or an interactive seminar, Angela customizes her material to impact your special group.

She offers participants a feast of insightful techniques to take home and her powerful message lives on, long after your event is over.

"Exceptional..." "Original..." "Inspirational..." "Wisdom that Warms the Heart"—is how her audience describes her. Clients range from Apple, Amex, Bell, Bombardier, Canada Trust, Goodyear, Ministry of the Attorney General, Sunnybrook Health Science Centre, Toyota to International Quality & Productivity Center, American Alliance, Sungard and Rogers.

To book Angela Jackson for your next conference or in-house event, please contact:

Angela Jackson Seminars
2693 Lakeshore Blvd West, Suite 11
Toronto, Canada, M8V 1G6
Telephone: 416-259-3365
Fax: 416-255-4635
E-mail: **angel.speak@sympatico.ca**
Website: **www.angelajackson.com**

We Have a Request...

Angela Jackson would love to hear how this book has affected you and members of your organization. Share your insights, stories and experiences. Do you have a tip or quote that you would like to offer other readers in Angela's popular newsletter *Sanity Savers*? Please send them to us, we want to hear from you!

Contact Angela at:

Angela Jackson Seminars
2693 Lakeshore Blvd West, Suite 11
Toronto, Canada, M8V 1G6
Telephone: 416-259-3365
Fax: 416-255-4635
E-mail: **angel.speak@sympatico.ca**
Website: **www.angelajackson.com**